Aliens, Unicorns

and

Executives...

It's Back to Business BASICs - Baby!

Michael Boch, CPA

Contents

Contents (continued)

Acknowledgments

To all of my bosses and their companies that I have worked for over the years – thank you. Thank you for hiring me and giving me the opportunity to work within these companies. For without these experiences, I never would have known that success is remote, at best, for nearly all, small businesses. Without those jobs, the BASIC Business Model™ would never have been conceived and this book never would have been completed.

To my Dad; thanks for instilling in me to find a career that I can be passionate for without any regard for its monetary rewards. After 43 years, I might have finally found it - to educate small business owners and executives.

To my Mom; thank you for the competitive and creative genes. They have served me well.

To Derian, Cailyn and Cameron, my children; thank you for your continuous zest for life. Each day brings me something new to laugh about and be proud of. I love you all very much.

To my wife, Terry, the kindest individual I know; thanks for your continued patience, support, love and friendship. I love you.

Introduction

We live in a strange and scary world. It can be even worse when you look only inside the world of business. No wonder so many businesses are struggling and failing, with the blame being placed squarely on a company's executives. The sad reality is that far too many executives are in over-their-head and they are simply not focusing on the critical business fundamentals within their respective departments.

According to the United States Small Business Administration ("USSBA") website, in 2003 there were 23.7 million small businesses which made up 99.7% of all employers. Additionally, the USSBA states that one half of all new employer firms survive less than four years. It seems that success in small business is exceptionally difficult. So why is it so tough? Well, it shouldn't be. The solution is simple and lies in getting back to boring *Business BASICs.*

As a Certified Public Accountant ("CPA") with over twenty-two years of professional experience, including nine years in public accounting, six of which were with a Big-Four CPA firm, and thirteen years in industry where I functioned as Controller or Chief Financial Officer for numerous small businesses, I have seen far too many problems consuming management and their companies. My experience with eighteen different industries has shown that the problems are not confined to only a few industries, but instead they are rampant throughout all. I have learned that the problems are not complex, but rather they can be easily resolved through Business 101 methodology – a.k.a. *Business BASICs.*

It wasn't until my fifth job in industry (my first four jobs were with companies losing money and in need of drastic change, in nearly all facets of their business) and after all those years in public that the light came on and it all became so crystal clear. Small businesses were dying and no one was around to help them. Within two weeks of arrival to my fifth industry position, I immediately noticed the same warning signals as in my past employment. I was amazed at how easy it was to spot potential problems – *and to help fix them*. This led me to the development of the ***BASIC Business Model*** ™. There is nothing scientific or statistical in its findings; just positive informative results. My focus groups were the companies that I was working for and trying to help. Since developing the Model, every small business that I have worked for, or come in contact with, has exhibited many of the same problem areas that the Model focuses on. Problems exist within all small businesses.

It's ironic that most individuals visit doctors for annual examinations; however, most companies never undergo a total annual diagnostic assessment to determine their overall state of business health. Sales, marketing, management, accounting, staffing, suppliers, customers, information systems, operations, and competition, are just some of the critical components to a company's long-term success. These are the vital signs of a business and they need to be monitored. Each of these components, if left untreated, can cripple a company.

The ***BASIC Business Model*** ™ is a qualitative, broad-based diagnostic paradigm that is designed to identify problems within specific areas of a small business. All of these areas, either directly or indirectly, can impact profitability, productivity, and/or the competitive position of a company.

BASIC is an acronym for the following components: **B**aseline Factors; **A**ccounting; **S**taffing; **I**nternal Processes; and the **C**hief Executive Officer. The twenty sub areas, or vital signs, within the *BASIC* components are:

- Baseline Factors: (customers, suppliers, competitors, and other external factors);
- Accounting: (cash and capital, reporting, internal accounting controls, and accounting resources);
- Staffing: (structure, rewards, fun and training);
- Internal Processes: (sales, marketing, operations and information systems); and
- Chief Executive Officer: (vision, communication, management, planning).

So if it is so easy to diagnose and fix problems why aren't more companies doing so? Answer: because the executive (a.k.a. CEO, President, vice-president of a department, owner, and/or founder) of the company is simply too busy putting out fires rather than searching for the root cause to the company's lack of productivity, competitive position or profitability. It becomes a vicious downward spiral until absolute panic and chaos sets in and by this time, it is simply too late to turn the company around. Oftentimes the executive is in a state of denial. Additionally, other executives and key subordinates within the company have few suggestions for improvement as they too have their own crisis issues. So if internal help is not available, what is the alternative?

The logical individual to help the executive is the company's outside CPA. After all, external CPAs market themselves as "valued business advisors." So where is the advice? Are they asleep at the corporate wheel? In some cases they are. Many CPAs that perform company audits or reviews are mainly concerned with just the numbers. It is purely quantitative results that are analyzed along with specific accounts, and this takes place usually months after year-end. Additionally, the financial information is stale by the time they present the financial report to management.

I submit that long before a company's Balance Sheet and Income Statement show any signs of problems, there are actually red flags blowing throughout an organization. You don't need to look at debits and credits to know that a company has significant problems. The outside CPA typically spends little or no time asking about non-financial information, so they are usually no help to the executive and client company when it comes to the dynamics affecting the business. Many CPAs working for public accounting firms have absolutely no idea what keeps the executive awake at night. Most of the time the executive views their external CPA as a traditional bean counter, without any knowledge of sales, marketing, operations, etc., and in the majority of cases, this is probably true. This leads to the executive rarely asking the CPA for business advice.

Other than perhaps saving some money from tax planning strategies, it is staggering how little value most CPA firms bring to their small business clients. This is because most of the face-to-face time that CPAs have with their clients is during the audit or review, where numbers, documentation and controls are everything. To be quite frank, the system is broken and doesn't allow the CPA much time to actually discuss the client's business strategies, challenges and threats, as resources are extremely thin. And with Sarbanes Oxley it will only get worse. Although internal accounting controls and processes are important, they are a very small percentage of the variables at work within a company. I did not fully realize this until I transitioned from public accounting to industry.

What about getting an industry or functional area consultant to aid the company? If you can find one that has produced results in the past at a reasonable price, then that is a good option. Just remember, most consultants are out-of-work company executives and are now trying to make a go of it on their own. They failed as internal executives but are now being paid as high priced consultants. Be careful and obtain references to confirm the consultant's effectiveness.

So if the external CPA and outside consultant are not necessarily the answer, then the executive has to arrive at a timely, valuable solution that is cost beneficial to her company. That solution can only be to find the time to zero in on the **Business BASICs.** *Aliens, Unicorns and Executives…It's Back to Business BASICs – Baby!* provides the executive with the key questions, by component area, geared to immediately highlight problem areas. Once diagnosed, simple action plans can be formulated to begin the transition of a company. Perfection is not the goal – focusing on the **BASICs** is.

In summary, **BASIC** business fundamentals, the critical ingredients of any successful business are often the most overlooked and under appreciated components of a business. Instead, most executives concentrate on the latest consulting trend or company crisis. For a company to ensure its continued long-term success, the future truly lies in getting back to *Business BASICs.* The executives are the only ones that can lead this charge. The next twenty chapters will provide a guide for the critical questions needed to be asked and why they are so important to a company's success. The *BASIC Business Model* ™ will greatly aid your efforts to your company's long-term success. Use it!

Part 1 - Baseline Factors

Baseline factors cover the four core external elements associated with any business:

1. **Customers,**

2. **Suppliers,**

3. **Competition, and**

4. **Other External Factors.**

For an enterprise to grow and prosper it is critical to monitor and understand the variables and dynamics of these four elements. Since they reside outside of the control environment of an entity's structure, the probability is much greater that one of the elements will negatively impact ones business.

Because of this risk uncertainty, it is imperative that these elements are treated as if they were part of a company's internal structure and processes. *Aliens, Unicorns and Executives...* serves to identify the potential financial and operational risks that a company may have. There are questions within each external element, that when answered honestly, can quickly diagnose problem areas that, if left unattended, can destroy a business.

CUSTOMERS

Customers are the heart of Baseline Factors. If "Cash is King", then the "Customer is Queen". If you are like most businesses, very little time is spent on a customer once they become a client of a company. Oftentimes, more time is spent trying to obtain a client than retain one. How does your company treat and deal with these queens? Does any one customer account for greater than 25% of total revenue? If so, what is your strategy for mitigating this risk? Do you annually prune your customer list, based upon a customer's profitability and/or strategic importance? Does the CEO meet annually with all the major clients at the CEO's request? How is pricing determined?

Each customer has a unique identify and needs. Understanding the dynamics surrounding one's customer is critical. Are your current customers suffocating your business? Is your service or product really what they want? Understanding the implications of these questions and your responses are critical to your business.

Does the CEO meet annually with key customers?

Usually it is only at the request of an irate customer, that the CEO makes a visit to their premises. The meeting is not a pleasant one for either party. Rarely does the CEO elect to visit key accounts on her own, but instead waits for problems. Think how powerful it would be for a CEO to just visit these key customers without an invitation for the sole purpose of saying "thank you for your business and how can we improve your satisfaction?" Take the time to learn more about what keeps your customers up at night. Their concern is your concern, because ultimately your company's success is dependant on theirs.

Are key accounts surveyed annually?

Although they are far less powerful than visiting a customer in person, annual surveys can obtain critical information at a much lower cost and quicker turnaround. Construct a customer survey with between 5 to 15 questions that are geared towards determining a customer's satisfaction with factors such as: the product, service, cost, delivery, quality, customer service, and any other factors or qualities that might be important. Ask some open-ended questions too, to allow for the customer to vent their frustrations. It is s good idea for the survey results to be sent directly to the CEO rather than a member of sales, marketing or customer service. If the reviewer is the CEO, then this shows that the customer relationship is truly valued and the survey has a better probability of getting returned.

Does any customer account for greater than 25% of total revenues, or do any two customers account for greater than 40%?

When starting a business, owners feel compelled to bring on new sales - no matter what the implications. This is especially true when the customer is prestigious or well known within the community or industry, since name recognition is important in customer referrals. Unfortunately having one or more significant revenue-producing clients usually drains even a higher percentage of the company's resources. If you haven't already done so, make sure you account for all overhead dollars when analyzing the profitability of this client.

Another factor that is even more difficult to quantify, is leverage. Leverage tends to side in the customer's favor; since they are in a position to hold the price, request a reduction, or simply go elsewhere. If you are in a commodity business, and most are – as I discuss later on in the book, then it's only a matter of time before these clients go elsewhere, and growth becomes stagnated due to resource depletion. Pay attention to your company's sales mix. Do not allow it to become highly distorted in terms of one or more significant customers. Remember to make the customer fit into your business processes without a lot of customization and hand holding. The results should show up directly in your bottom-line.

Is the customer list pruned annually?

The best thing you can do for your competitors is to give them your problem accounts; most of which are probably consuming an inordinate amount of your company's resources. If you were able to fully capture all the costs associated with these accounts, then the likelihood that they were actually costing you more than the revenue generated would be extremely high. Each year, the customer list should be reviewed and pruned.

Customers that are of strategic importance; have strong growth potential; are in a "hot" market; or are considerably profitable should obviously be retained. All others are best to be sent to your fiercest competitor. Additionally, in some cases it may even be worth it to send some problem, profitable accounts to your competition since they can significantly drain the morale out of your staff – and replacing experienced and productive employees can be extremely costly. Start quantifying the non-billable time being spent on certain accounts and make a decision to prune back. This also gives your staff the time to focus on your more valuable customers and new opportunities.

Is the customer sometimes wrong?

Yes, the customer is, in fact, sometimes wrong. The plain truth is that sometimes the best thing you can do for your competition is to give them some of your problematic and unprofitable accounts. If a customer is consuming a great deal of your company's resources, chances are you are losing money on this account. Taking the approach that the customer is always right can cost your company a great deal of money.

Certainly there are those customers that may be unprofitable, but from a strategic sense, they are worth kissing up too. Additionally, the earlier a company is in its lifecycle the more support it needs to give its clients. As a company grows, it should become choosier in its client retention. Remember – there are probably a handful of clients that are far too demanding for the value that they bring. Either increase their pricing significantly or pass them on to your competitors – and don't look back!

COMPETITORS

Competitors provide the uncertainty and ulcers within the Baseline Factors. How well do you really know your competition? Unless you are in professional sports and receive frequent scouting reports on the opposition, you probably know very little. Think about the time spent analyzing opposing players in major league and college sports. Now think about how much time your management team spends analyzing competitors. This is a huge factor in why your business is not hitting its financial, sales and operational goals. If the CEO and his or her management team cannot name three strengths and weaknesses of the top five competitors, then your business has a serious problem and is undoubtedly wasting valuable resources.

For any company to suggest that they have created a barrier to enter because of their technology, patent, or first to market - then they certainly don't understand what a truly global technological race we are in. A race where there is plenty of capital just waiting for that new revolutionary idea that will make your once golden product an obsolete albatross. Have you recently wondered what Burt next door was building in his garage? Understanding the implications of these questions and your responses are critical to your business.

Can senior management and the sales team members name the top five competitors?

Every member of the sales team, along with the CEO and all members of senior management, should be able to name the top five competitors and know a great deal about each. Oftentimes you will hear a CEO mention, "We really don't have any competitors." This is a tell tale sign that he has not spent enough time: researching the market; talking to customers; talking to his attorneys, bankers or accountants; or talking to his sales staff. Additionally, this arrogance and ignorance is a giant red flag that this person should probably not be running a company. Don't be stupid! Every company has competitors and threats of substitute products, or services, which could easily put you out-of-business.

Can the CEO and sales team members name three strengths of each major competitor?

A business should know the strengths and weaknesses of all its major competitors. It may actually benefit your company to try and guess at your competitor's overall strategies. Without this knowledge, a business is immediately at a significant disadvantage with its current customers and within the marketplace. The risk of losing market share can be extremely high.

In sports, it is a common practice for coaches and players to thoroughly know each particular facet of an opposing team. What are the team's strengths? What players dominate? What is the normal game plan or strategy for this team? Where are they most vulnerable? Do they run the ball; shoot from three point range; like to hit and run; send only two men into the opposing zone; or always pass on the inside rail?

By predicting and understanding another's strategy, the odds of beating that opponent are greatly increased. In business the odds are even better, because the game lasts much longer than a few hours. Accordingly, luck can be largely eliminated from the equation. It will come down to the game plan and execution, not just the raw skill level of the players.

Is management open to acquisitions with competitors?

One of the most common ways of growing a business in the 90's, and it continues to be today, is through acquisitions and/or mergers, but yet a majority of companies never actually see this strategy to fruition. Oftentimes the founder or CEO simply think her company is too small to consider an acquisition. Remember, deals can be structured in numerous ways, and you do not have to acquire an entire company. You could instead buy a customer base, intellectual asset, tangible assets, or whatever other facet is deemed to add value to one's business.

Other times, the CEO believes that her company will grow only internally, and why acquire another business since it has its own series of problems. For whatever the reason, the reality of having a dual growth strategy – internal and by acquisition – still makes sense in today's market and can create enormous value and opportunity. In addition, it puts the competition on notice that you are an entity to be reckoned with, and as such, many will actually approach you to buy them. Remember, "Image is everything," so let the competitors think you are larger than you truly are.

Does senior management bad-mouth the competition?

There is nothing worse than hearing a top executive bad mouth the competition. It is much wiser to bite your tongue and have at least one or two kind words about them. Every company has some good qualities, just as they have some bad ones. How much validity is there in a statement criticizing a company that has been around for ten years, saying that they have a lousy product or service? They must be doing something right to have been around for those years.

Instead highlight why your product or service is so valuable to the potential customer. In most cases the product or service being sold is a commodity anyway, even though executives might view it differently. It is tough to differentiate a commodity, so why bad-mouth a competitor. "I'm sure they are good and they have certainly been around longer than us, but we feel we are better for the following reasons . . . ", is a professional response and one that your potential customer will respect.

Is the Company susceptibility to global competition?

Any CEO that believes his company's product or service is not susceptible to global competition, does not understand the nature of today's business dynamics and the ease with which a product or service can be brought to market. No doubt there are the exceptions, but there are few of these. One of the greatest problems facing a small business is that it can't possibly account for all its competitors and new substitute products about to enter the market.

Every business is susceptible to both the guy in the garage next-door, working in secret; as it is to the foreign unknown competitor trying to enter a new territory. Don't be in denial regarding this matter. Take care of your customers and the competition will have a much harder time gaining share.

SUPPLIERS

Suppliers can bring a company's operations to a screeching halt; and, for that reason alone, are a critical component of Baseline factors. Suppliers should be treated as though their makeup is a combination of customer and competition. It is imperative that one respects them as a customer, but also takes the time to understand their strengths and weaknesses, like one would a competitor. If your company selects suppliers based solely on cost, then prepare yourself for the inevitable problems associated with quality, delivery, timeliness, reputation, and other setbacks typical of using a low cost provider. It is rare that the lowest price ticket provides one with the best view of the game.

Has your company developed an overall grading system for its major suppliers? Are there emergency backup suppliers available, should your main vendors suddenly experience operational difficulties? Has your company outgrown your supplier's capacity or are you about to get eliminated from your supplier's customer list? Understanding the implications of these questions and your responses are critical to your business.

Has the company developed and implemented an overall grading system for major suppliers?

Suppliers of products, services, and information are an integral part of any business. Without them, you would have no customers. As such, due diligence on all major suppliers should be performed to ensure that the actual total supplier cost is reasonable and within the contracted specifications. Due diligence should typically include monitoring: cost, quality, reliability, turnaround time, financial stability, accessibility, reputation, and location. Although cost is certainly the most easily quantifiable factor, the others have a far greater potential effect on a company's profitability, productivity, and competitive positioning.

Identifying inefficiencies and hidden costs resulting from elements other than cost, are crucial to accurately determine a supplier's true total cost. Create several key metrics and track them monthly, making sure that the supplier is within an acceptable range. Remember, you are your suppliers' customer. Make sure you are treated as such!

Is annual financial information on major suppliers requested?

Key suppliers play an integral part in the success of a business. If delivers are consistently late or quality is extremely poor, that can cripple a company's success and damage its reputation. The worst possibility is to have a key supplier be on the brink of financial collapse and for your business to not even realize it.

Businesses are programmed to request financial information on potential new customers to check their credit, yet rarely do these same businesses request financial data on key suppliers. It is worth repeating; you are your suppliers' customers and should be treated as such. If they really want your business, then they will provide you with financial data that can be used to assess their stability. Take appropriate measures to determine that your key supplier's are solvent. If they are low cost but are at risk of going out of business, then find another supplier. Requesting financial data should be an annual process – don't ignore this important risk management process.

Does the Company monitor subcontractor utilization?

In today's business environment, it is commonplace for companies to utilize subcontractors for all facets of the business. To allow routine and/or complex processes to be performed by other companies can make good business sense. But to not closely monitor the subcontractor will, in most cases, end in project overruns or inferior work.

Before the contract is executed, project deliverables along with a detailed project timeline, should be agreed to by both parties. Weekly status reports should be prepared showing problems encountered and changes to originally planned deadline dates should be reported and approved. Project changes usually will always have an adverse effect on the bottom-line forecast. Always, always, always, be sure that there is an internal manager responsible for the subcontractor relationship and that this manager has adequate experience in the process or project outsourced. Otherwise, the subcontractor may take advantage of the relationship and fees will begin to escalate.

Is low cost often the most important issue when selecting a supplier?

Quit constantly searching for the lowest price – it simply is not worth your time. Oftentimes the product or service will be inferior, ending up costing you even more in resource consumption. There should be many factors, other than cost, to consider when deciding on which vendor to purchase from, among them are: reputation of the vendor, quality, timeliness of delivery, cost, years in business, size of the company, financial stability, and location to name a few.

Think about the importance of the item as it relates to the overall success of your business, and let that be an indicator of what other factors should be considered.

Are there emergency back up suppliers available?

Having backup suppliers ready and available to delivery key products or services is crucial in running a business. If anything should happen to your main supplier your business will not miss a beat, and any impact on your customers will be minimal. A better risk management solution would be to allow a second supplier a smaller portion of your business on a continued basis. That way it keeps the primary supplier honest in its delivery terms and provides your business with insurance incase the primary supplier ever experiences any severe problems. It also allows the secondary vendor to become familiar with your business and needs.

Companies forced to search in a panic for new key vendors may find that the new vendor can simply not establish the relationship quick enough. This leaves your company vulnerable to potential customer delays and problems that will undoubtedly impact your customers and profits.

OTHER EXTERNAL FACTORS

Other External Factors are the most overlooked of a company's Baseline Factors. As a result, a company is oftentimes venerable to a host of peripheral elements that in time can contribute to an entity's collapse and failure. Although these elements are continuously at play outside of the business, they oftentimes can indirectly affect the daily activities and culture within an organization. Being in touch with the dynamics and variables of external factors can provide a competitive advantage to an attentive company. For instance, does your company have a plan to deal with the greatest demographic issue facing it? Does it even know what that issue is? What is the number one threat to your company's product or service? How does the community feel about the Company, its CEO and the employees? Have the events of September 11, 2001 changed the way your company operates?

Taking the time to assess the risk associated with external factors, and to develop and execute action plans to mitigate this risk, will ultimately prove as a key differentiator over your competition. In the long-term, your company should gain market share and increase its profitability. How long do you think it will be before they create a union in your business sector? Understanding the implications of these questions and your responses are critical to your business.

Is there a plan to deal with the greatest demographic issue facing the company?

Typically not only do most companies not have a plan for attacking the most pressing demographic issue facing it, but most do not even know what the issue is. A company must understand the communities and demographics that it deals within; especially those on its own turf. Whether they are changes to the average age of the population; taxes; income; unemployment percentage; lack of a skilled or non-skilled work force; schools; or a poor infrastructure; all of these can create enormous roadblocks and divergence to a company's current strategy.

Paying attention to these demographic variables and characteristics can allow a Company to stake claim to a competitive advantage or accurately diagnose a market disadvantage. Take time to understand those factors outside of your company's internal structure.

Is the Company's product or service considered a commodity or value-added?

In some form or other, the Internet has changed the way nearly every business conducts itself along with the markets it choices to operate in. Technology as a whole has simply brought the competition much closer. Because of this, there are actually very few companies that truly have a product or service that can be considered a non-commodity.

First movers in an industry surely are not selling a commodity, but nearly all businesses, whether the CEO admits it or not, are marketing a commodity. As such, strategies should be developed that are more in line with a commodity business, as opposed to marketing a value-added product or service business. Be aware of the true value of your product or service and it will probably aid in the process of the company's strategic decisions.

Is there union activity?

Unions served a tremendous purpose in earlier days; however, with the number of opportunities available in today's world, businesses understand that union or no union, they must be competitive in wages, benefits and the demands placed on their workforce. With a lot of work being contracted to overseas partners, there is a likelihood that unions will begin to form again. Pay attention to what is happening in your industry and that of others.

Unions can create a huge risk for the business and its owners. Given the power of a unified body, it has the potential to almost cripple a business overnight. If your business is unionized or you suspect union activity, senior management should take every measure to ensure that contingency plans can be quickly implemented in the event that a union strikes.

Is the "word on the street" positive?

If the "word on the street" is positive, chances are your company is doing many things right. As such, potential customers will seek you out; the competition's employees will want to work for you; and suppliers will recognize the long-term opportunities from doing business with you, and therefore, possibly offer more favorable terms as incentive for contracting with them. It is certainly a snowball effect going up, but can be an avalanche coming down.

Many factors can contribute to the market's perception of the company, but the one that is of utmost importance and of low cost to implement, is having a corporate culture whereby everyone is treated fairly and with respect. This professionalism will ultimately pay huge, long-term dividends. Don't forget, the "word on the street" is largely communicated and initiated by the employees at your Company. Make sure it is favorable communication.

Does senior management consider the business to be complex?

Show me a CEO or manager that states, "That doesn't work for our business; our business is too complex," and I'll show you a non-creative, confused person.

Businesses should not be complex. They are all working with the same fundamental principals trying to grow their company. It is a wise and experienced person that can quickly break down various processes and concepts into simplified forms. Without this exceptional trait, a business will be buried in details and seem extremely complex and problem oriented. If you company isn't building a rocket to travel to mars – chances are you don't have a complex business. Keep things simple – and your business should flourish.

Part 2 - Accounting

Accounting covers the four critical areas within a business' financial discipline:

1. **Cash and Capital,**
2. **Accounting Resources,**
3. **Reporting, and**
4. **Internal Accounting Controls.**

Although most entrepreneurs and CEO's of small businesses equate accounting with debits equaling credits; there is so much more to this vital element. The adage that "Cash is King" can only be truly appreciated by those companies that have experienced financial hardship - and there are scores of them. How many key performance operational and financial measures is your company tracking on a monthly basis? Is an Accounting Clerk, Office Manager, Certified Public Accountant, or a recent college graduate minding the books? How active is your Board of Directors?

This section serves to identify the potential problems common to a company's financial, treasury, risk management, and strategic planning areas. There are questions within each critical area, that when answered honestly, can quickly diagnose specific problem areas that, if left unattended, can quite possibly cripple a business.

CASH AND CAPITAL

Cash and capital are the most critical components to growing a business. They are at the core of the BASIC Business Model's™ second fundamental area – "Accounting". A small business can never have enough cash and capital. They are the lifelines to success. As critical to a business as these elements are, most businesses do not even have a cash-forecasting model in place. Because of this they are totally unaware as to whether the business could weather a sudden and severe decline. Does your company have a plan for raising emergency funds? Is there only one option? Remember, the best time to secure financing is when you do not need it. So it is imperative for management to stay ahead of its creditors and bankers.

When trying to raise capital what method will management use to value the company? Is it consistent with the method used by industry experts? How does the founder and/or majority shareholder feel about dilution and stock valuation? Answers to these questions will dictate whether the company will in fact be able to weather a business downturn. Do you know your company's monthly burn rate? Get your hands around cash now – before it is too late.

Are cash flow projections prepared on a 3, 6 and 12 month basis, and revised quarterly?

"Cash is King!" This is especially true with small and midsize companies. An organization is most venerable to market and competitive pressures when there is inadequate cash to support business operations, debt service, and future growth. Having enough cash and capital is absolutely paramount to the long-term success of any business. It is equally important to fully understand what your cash needs are within a given period. Why then, do so many companies fail to prepare short-term cash forecasts? A forecast is an essential tool that enables a business to properly plan for its organizational and operational needs. Short-term forecasts usually consist of twelve weekly periods, while a long-term forecast should consist of at least four quarterly periods. Subsequent to a year, forecasts should be annualized. Critically important in preparing a forecast is to capture, and reasonably estimate, all potential cash inflows and outflows over a given period. Without a forecasting model, a company runs the risk that one-day could unexpectedly be its last day.

Be proactive and understand your cash needs ahead of time. Make cash forecasting a routine, high-priority process within your organization, so that you too can perhaps avoid desperate measures. Management and the company loose any leverage it had, once the cash closes in on empty. Don't be lazy! Monitor your cash situation closely.

Is there sufficient cash and capital to weather a financial storm?

Not having adequate cash and capital reserves to weather a sudden and severe business decline can leave a company desperate and without any leverage. The resulting financing, whether from angel investors, venture capitalists, or even a bank, will usually come at a much higher premium. Most parties will sense the desperation and play a waiting game with the company's founder, looking to obtain a much higher percentage of the company for a lot less dollars. Companies should consistently plan for having at least enough cash or credit available to cover six to nine months of operations. This way, in the event of a business disaster, the company can continue in business long enough to determine what viable options to remedy the downturn. Without enough working capital the company is at the mercy of the markets and in all likelihood will be forced into drastic business changes and perhaps even bankruptcy.

Does any one shareholder own greater than fifty percent?

When one shareholder owns greater than fifty percent of the company, there is a tendency for that person to make decisions that are for the good of that individual as opposed to for the good of the company. Control can be costly. The individual, typically the founder/CEO, will often refer to the company as his or her company. This can greatly deflate the morale of the employees as it can lead them to believe that their hard work is strictly for the benefit of the founder. So many founders are absolutely consumed with retaining the majority of stock so that when the big bucks come they will have the majority to cash out.

The sad reality is that far too often, if at all, the truly big bucks will likely not come until the founder has diluted himself below fifty percent. This is when the venture capitalists will begin to view the company not as a mom and pop business, but an entity where the founder will not be able to veto certain business decisions because it is a personal issue. Founders have to be willing to give up control. In the majority of cases the founder never gives up control and the big bucks never come.

Are there several viable options on raising emergency funds?

The best time to consider raising emergency funds is when your company doesn't need cash, not when it's close to bankruptcy. If one waits to long, there will be no leverage left to either borrow funds or sell stock to raise funds at reasonable terms.

Entrepreneurs should have several viable options on raising emergency funds; in fact, it is best to actually raise enough cash to cover an unexpected business downturn. Take advantage of setting up credit lines and other facilities before the balance sheet begins to deteriorate. Parties are much more apt to execute lending agreements, and invest in the Company, when business is good, not when the lights are beginning to dim and the phones have been disconnected. Companies should use every measure available to survive against turbulent times unless, off course, there are other major holes in the company's business model and plan. If this is the case, cash will not solve the problem. Instead, the Company should probably hire a turnaround expert or consult with an experienced business advisor.

Is the method used to value the company consistent with that used within the industry?

Founders and CEO's are notorious for believing that their companies are worth millions and millions based upon some crazy business valuation that is not the norm within their respective industry. It is this reason alone why so many entrepreneurs never realize their dreams and fail to see the pot of gold.

Greed oftentimes strangles the CEO's thinking. When valuing your company, use valuation methods that are consistent with those used to value competitors operating in your same markets. Also, a key point to remember is that if 100 venture capitalists were asked to value a business, there would probably be 100 different valuation ranges, but their methods of valuation and the range itself would be fairly consistent. Don't be greedy!

ACCOUNTING RESOURCES

Accounting resources, for small businesses, are usually dependant on the Controller or Chief Financial Officer (even with the title they often perform some lower level tasks). This individual needs to be a hands-on person, with not only an understanding of debits and credits, but he or she must have excellent business acumen. Most founders, CEO's, and entrepreneurs ignore the value of a strong Controller. Instead, they view the Controller as nothing but a person to perform the monthly close.

How involved in the company is your Controller? Is she asked to participate in meetings on pricing decisions, human resource concerns, contract renewal, operational issues, or strategic planning, to name just a few? Or, is the Controller nothing but a "yes" person? If your Controller has a combination of public accounting and industry experience, and is a CPA, chances are she has seen numerous business settings, problems, and transactions, and is probably more adept at formulating solutions and strategy than most of your management team. Are your company's accounting resources being adequately utilized, or did you hire the first accounting person that applied? Remember, you get what you pay for.

Have you done a complete background check on the Controller and/or CFO?

Once the candidate has passed through the main face-to-face interview process the company should now perform some key due diligence before a final offer can be extended. Checking references and performing a background check is a necessity in order to ensure that there are no major skeletons hanging out. The heads of your accounting and finance departments are in the best position to commit fraud - if they wish. Think of it as handing over the keys to your car and house to a stranger.

It is absolutely imperative that complete background checks be performed on any new accounting people that are in a position to perpetrate fraud. Without proper due diligence, the company eventually ends up paying much more in dealing with problem employees and the cost of fraud may never be fully known. In small businesses, the problems that a troublesome or fraudulent employee brings to the workplace can be crippling to the business. Take the added precaution and get confirmation on the achievements and background of your next accounting hire.

Is the number one accounting person a Certified Public Accountant ("CPA")?

When analyzing the qualifications of the number one accounting person within a small business, perhaps the most important qualification is for that individual to be a CPA. The skills of a CPA should provide the owner and CEO with a sense of security, technical knowledge and professionalism that a CPA brings. Having passed the uniform exam, it is clear that the CPA has a high level of technical skills, which can greatly benefit the company when complex situations and problems arise.

A CPA is trained to act as a business advisor and that is precisely what a small business needs most. To have a CPA employed can be a tremendous advantage to any company. An ideal background for a Controller is to be a CPA that has worked both in public accounting and also in industry. The experienced gained from these positions will be invaluable to the founder, CEO and the Company.

Is the number one accounting person heavily involved in business decisions?

Unfortunately, many CEO's and founders think of accountants as simply "bean counters," unable to add value unless it relates to an accounting issue. The reality is, CPA's and experienced CFOs or Controllers are exactly whom the CEO should be discussing most, if not all, high level decisions with, for several reasons. Firstly, most

CPA's, especially those that have worked in public accounting, have observed many businesses and therefore can quickly spot financial "red flag" areas. Secondly, by nature they are conservative and therefore provide a good compliment to most sales and marketing oriented CEO's. Thirdly, every decision made either directly or indirectly impacts the numbers, and because of this the CPA should be somewhat involved in all significant decisions. Having the knowledge of future events, allows the CPA to more accurately forecast cash – which is the most critical process in business. In summary, most CPAs working within industry are exceptionally qualified and thoroughly understand the dynamics of business.

Is the top accountant a "yes" person?

Although it is certainly an asset to have a CPA in the management group, it is not good if that CPA is always a "yes" person. Whoever the top accountant is, it does not do any good for the business to have a person in that position agreeing all the time. Accountants are risk adverse by nature; quite different from their peers in sales, marketing and operations. Oftentimes it is the accountant that is the lone holdout in many strategic decisions. Although they may be right as often as they are wrong, they at least should challenge the ideas of other members of management.

Things are never quite as rosy as they seem, and it is up to the top accountant within an organization to point this out. If accountants are always saying yes, yes, yes; and go, go, go, this could be a bad mix of decision makers. If your top accountant is always in agreement with you, it might be time to hire a replacement. This might be the first time you hear a "no" from your accountant.

Is there an adequate segregation of duties within key account areas?

In many small businesses it is difficult to have an adequate segregation of duties among the accounting personnel because there typically are not enough staff. However, there are mitigating controls that can and must be implemented to strengthen the accounting environment. For companies that have only one or two accounting personnel, one mitigating control is to have the CEO play a much more active role in reviewing the key account monthly reconciliation's such as cash, inventory and accounts receivable. Occasionally ask to see the bank statement and review the checks that have cleared, making sure to account for all of them. Review the accounts receivable aging making note of significantly past due accounts. Make sure that there are adequate procedures in place to safeguard the company's physical assets like inventory and computer equipment.

The CEO should also ask for a vendor listing or check disbursement register, so that if any of the names are unfamiliar an inquiry can be made. For those companies where there are more accounting personnel, it is much easier to have an adequate segregation of duties, but the CEO should still be close enough to the cash, so he or she has a better chance at catching any potential errors or irregularities.

REPORTING

Reporting is another one of the basic fundamentals in Accounting; however, it should go well beyond simply reporting a monthly income statement and balance sheet. Reporting should include a report card on all the key performance indicators ("KPIs") within each facet of a company. How many KPIs does your company track for sales, human resources, operations, marketing, information systems and other critical areas of a business? Is an annual operating budget prepared and are monthly meetings held with department heads to review significant variances? How timely are the reports given to management?

Without an accurate, timely and all encompassing reporting system, a company's management team is at a significant disadvantage. How well would our troops do in a battle without timely intelligence to aid in their efforts. By not providing critical feedback on all disciplines of a business, the chances for future growth and profitability are remote at best. What are your company's key success factors?

Is a key performance indicator report, monitoring all the key success factors within each department, prepared monthly?

Having a monthly, key performance indicator report is a critical management tool that provides a monthly pulse on all the vital signs of a company. Think of it as if you were in school, working on your grade point average ("GPA"). Each course is equally important in its overall impact on your GPA. Although the courses are dramatically different in scope; if you falter in one course, it drastically decreases your chances of ultimate success. The same is true in business.

Monitoring the key performance indicators will reveal trends and problem areas within each discipline of the business. Management can then initiate action plans to curtail further problems. Once you have started tracking the key performance indicators only then will you be able to accurately respond to whether your company would receive a passing grade.

Is the month end close by the fifth business day?

We are long past the days of manual spreadsheets and punch cards. Small businesses that are not able to close their monthly books within five business days need to find a new Controller or CFO. It is simply not worth the time to ensure 100% accuracy on the monthly financial statements, and any Controller that believes otherwise, is buried in details and is probably not adding much value to the overall business. It is far better to utilize accruals for major account areas and adjust later in the month when actual figures are known. A tighter close (by the tenth business day) can be performed at quarter end.

Timely generation of reasonable and reliable financial information for management is critical for effective decision-making. It is absolutely not necessary for monthly financials to be 100% accurate as this would create significant reporting delays. You are always going to have situations that arise where something was missed. The key is to have processes that will catch it and a good forecasting and budgeting system in place to compare actual results to planned results. If a

Controller has sound organizational and reporting skills, and has developed some key metric reporting, and has a good sense of the business, he or she can close a month within a few days. Real-time financial reporting is no longer an impossible dream.

Are monthly reporting packages delivered to management on a timely basis?

It is absolutely imperative that management receives a monthly reporting package on a timely basis, so that decisions can be made and any new strategies formulated.

The reporting package should contain key performance measures for the current month versus projected results and the prior months. The reporting package should be distributed to all senior managers within ten days after the monthly close (fifteen days for the quarterly close). Most small businesses fail to gather and communicate this critical decision making data to the individuals needing it the most – the managers. For the few that do prepare reports, oftentimes the data is communicated a month or two later, making it difficult to use the dated data constructively. It is up to the Controller to make this happen. Be sure to hold him or her accountable for this critical process.

Is there a reliable forecasting model and process in place?

Preparing a forecast that is reasonable and achievable is one of the most difficult tasks for management, yet having a reliable forecasting model is essential to running a business. Without one, it is nearly impossible to make decisions associated with personnel, capital expenditures, cash and other critical resources. Many small businesses start the forecasting process by arbitrarily arriving at a top-line revenue number followed by a bottom line desired net income amount and then fill in the middle. This is doomed for failure from the beginning.

Ideally the management team should take time to arrive at the two most critical volume assumptions associated with a forecast: sales and capacity - which can limit sales volume. To arrive at a reasonable sales figure, research should be conducted on: the expected overall market growth; competitor analysis; discussions with sales and management individuals; new product development and the timing of bringing it to market; review of the current customer base; and the company's historic growth rates. Regarding capacity, the Company has historical information on its resource capacity – both equipment and people. Once sales and capacity are determined, management can begin the process of projecting both variable and fixed expenses. Remember, once a forecast is complete; it is imperative to compare the actual monthly results to plan and make any necessary changes to ensure that expenses and cash outflows stay in line with actual sales. Finally, don't be overly optimistic in your forecasts!

Is there an accurate cost accounting system?

If a company, whether service or manufacturing, does not have an accurate cost accounting system then they will never truly be able to make sound strategic business decisions. Without accurate cost reporting it is impossible to know which products and services are profitable and which should be discontinued.

Besides capturing all variable costs, it is more critical to allocate fixed costs, as well as those that are semi-variable in nature, to a product or service. The more accurate your allocation of non-variable costs to the product, the more precise your margin analyses will be; allowing management's decision making on pricing and discontinuing of products to be more effective. Take the time to have your Controller provide management with a detailed accountability of all costs, but first be sure to provide your Controller with the necessary resources to perform this important task. This will make for a far more profitable business capable of beating its competitors and sustaining growth.

INTERNAL ACCOUNTING CONTROLS

Internal accounting controls at most small businesses consist only of monthly bank reconciliations and an occasional collection call to a customer. To mitigate the possibility of fraud, theft and collusion, all areas within a company need controls surrounding them. Without internal accounting controls a company is allowing its competitors to gain an advantage, either directly or indirectly; and it can quickly find itself in a precarious position.

Companies should utilize both internal and external controls. Does your company have a Board of Directors with at least two outside members? Is an annual audit performed? Is there an annual shareholder meeting allowing for questions and answers? Does the cost accounting system provide accurate and timely cost data? Are background checks performed on new management and employees?

Has your company taken every precaution to protect each department's assets, both tangible and intellectual? Founders rarely take time to adequately protect a company's assets, but instead dwell on the cost of purchasing a fire proof safe. It's just a matter of time before assets are stolen, destroyed, or inadvertently lost. Put controls in place now to safeguard your company's assets.

Is an annual operating budget prepared and are monthly meetings held to discuss variances?

The annual operating budget is an essential financial control mechanism for any business, providing the foundation for controlling expenses. Without it, there is no vehicle for quickly recognizing, and subsequently reducing, escalating monthly costs and losses.

Developing an operating budget is an educational process for everyone involved. Although the process is not difficult, it can be time consuming. The operating budget is developed once the actual sales forecast has been submitted and agreed to by the senior management team. For preparing the budget, one person, usually the Controller, or President if no Controller exists, should act as the facilitator. The budget must be reasonable and achievable. Do not force the numbers just for the sake of showing greater forecasted profits. For this reason, the Controller is a better person to facilitate than the President. The Controller should bring an independent, conservative and professional approach to the entire process. Off course, no budget should be final until the Board approves it.

Does the company utilize at least three key external controls?

Having external control measures in place will show any potential investor, the company's employees, and the founder, that the management team is serious about running a professional company. Oftentimes the CEO and founder is the same individual, and by having a Board of Directors in place serves as the greatest external oversight function within a business. It forces accountability of the CEO – a critical ingredient of success if a small business is to grow. For companies without an outside Board, it is usually because the CEO fears failure.

Although there is no absolute rule, a company should consider having an audit if revenue exceeds fifteen million. Although audits are not designed to confirm and verify the majority of transactions, they do serve, as a much needed company-wide oversight. Additionally, if your accounting staff is weak, you might find that having an audit will drastically change the financial statements due to incorrect accounting from complex transactions. If the revenue is less than fifteen million, a review will usually suffice. Lastly, quarterly communications to investors show that the management team is not trying to hide results and is open to comments and suggestions from its investors. By communicating on a regular basis, the company has a far greater chance of obtaining more finance should it need more capital. External controls demonstrate to all stakeholders that management, particularly the CEO, is willing to be held accountable for the financial results.

Are timely monthly reconciliations performed on all key accounts?

There is absolutely no reason (including time constraints), for not performing timely monthly reconciliation's on key accounts such as inventory, cash, accounts receivable, deferred revenue, accounts payable and other accounts deemed to be of a critical nature for the business. If your accounting staff is not performing reconciliation's it is certainly grounds for a formal warning or even eventual termination.

There is nothing more embarrassing than to explain to your Board of Directors and other stakeholders that the year-to-date results were wrong because inventory was grossly misstated or accounts receivable were never reconciled. The credibility of management is immediately brought into question, as management is the one that is ultimately held accountable. Reconciliation's are a critical part of accounting and must be completed regularly or management should be ready to face the consequences.

Does the CEO understand how to interpret the monthly financial results?

Most CEO's have a business background in sales, marketing, human resources or some sort of technical expertise. Rarely do CEO's have a Finance or Accounting background. As such, many are not proficient with reading and understanding financial statements. There is more to reviewing financial statements than just seeing the revenue numbers and bottom-line figures. Statements of Cash Flows show the inflows and outflows of cash and provide a powerful tool for where cash is being generated from or used for. Additionally, review of the Balance Sheet can quickly indicate a company's solvency through noting their working capital, debt and equity sections.

The CEO that takes the time to understand the financials, and what drives those numbers, has a much better sense for any strategic changes that need to be made. There are plenty of one or two day courses for non-financial managers. It is in your company's best interest for all non-financial executives to attend.

Are capital expenditures financially justified?

For all significant capital expenditures, a company must be able to justify the expenditure based upon some rate of return, payback period or operational necessity. Simply purchasing a new machine or piece of equipment because it has the latest technology is a poor business decision by any manager.

Capital expenditures should be budgeted annually in the capital budget and the capital budget should be tied directly to the strategic initiatives of the business. Capital expenditure decisions should also be based with long range planning in mind, not a one or two-year outlook. Certainly there are those expenditures that may make sense to upgrade annually, but they are very few and usually are not a significant portion of the overall budget. For larger dollar items, be sure that you understand the market in which your company operates and anticipate what changes may be coming over the next two to five years, before any decision is made. Oftentimes your vendors can give you a good idea of the next generation of products or services. Once all the facts are collected and digested, then decide whether to purchase, lease or wait.

Part 3 - Staffing

Staffing deals with the four essentials necessary to ensure a productive and enthusiastic workforce:

1. **Training,**

2. **Structure,**

3. **Fun, and**

4. **Rewards.**

For an enterprise to grow and prosper, it is critical to monitor and understand the variables and dynamics of these four elements. Since these elements are internal in nature, they should be much easier to control, allowing for a company to continually improve upon its core staffing area. Does your company seem to be in a constant state of disarray? Are your employees happy or burnt out? Is training considered a key to gaining a competitive advantage? The BASIC Business Model™ serves to identify the potential financial and operational risks that a company may have.

TRAINING

Training is absolutely critical to a company's long-term success, but most businesses have a tendency to ignore this most fundamental need. What percentage of revenues does your company budget for training? When's the last time your VP of Business Development attended a seminar on, say, strategic partnering? Does the CEO consider training to be trivial or crucial to the prosperity of the business? One does not have to journey to an outside facility, but rather, the company can develop internal departmental and company-wide training sessions for everyone. Management, including the CEO, also needs annual training to develop new skills, and sharpen those that are currently being utilized.

Training serves not only to increase an individual's productivity, but it sends an invaluable message to the employee; the Company wants to invest in your future! This serves to boast ones confidence in performing his duties and ultimately builds a more loyal worker.

Does the CEO consider training critical to the long-term success of the company?

If yes, that's great. Developing the skills to perform one's job can only be achieved through adequate training and experience. Oftentimes it boils down to the CEO simply not placing a priority on training, and seeing it as nothing more than overhead, without any payback.

As an organization's strategy changes due to industry and market pressures, and with the ever-changing technological advances, it is imperative that a company requires, and supports, training for all levels. It not only serves to enhance an individual's skills - thus increasing productivity - but it heightens a person's confidence and self-esteem. This is especially the case with staff members. For senior executives, training provides a much-needed refresher course on critical skills needed to drive the business forward. Give employees the tools to perform and, through productivity gains, your company will beat the competition - providing the company with its greatest payback.

Are training costs actually budgeted for in the annual operating plan?

One factor supporting a CEO's statement that she believes training is crucial to an employee's advancement and productivity is to incorporate training into the company's overall operating budget. If training is to be truly thought of as critical, then it should be budgeted for on a departmental basis for all employees.

In today's drastically changing and challenging business environment, it is the companies that continually develop the skills of their employees and managers that eventually outperform the competition. For the companies that occasionally send an employee or two to a course only because the employee requested it and the company fears losing that employee, they are greatly limiting that employee's potential which ultimately will impact the company's profitability and competitive positioning. If employees believe that you want to provide them with greater skills and knowledge, they will be much more loyal to your company; making for a more productive workforce.

Do key staff, managers and the CEO have annual training?

All key staff, including the management team and CEO should have some form of annual training. With business becoming increasingly more dynamic, it is imperative that the people responsible for creating the strategy and managing the people have some annual training on the latest business paradigms of successful companies. In addition, the training can serve as valuable refresher courses in the disciplines that they are responsible for. Lastly, departmental superstars, the ones that will be your next managers, need to be groomed and continually trained. Rather than grooming them in your ways, mix in some formal training through outside experts. It is well worth the investment.

Is an individual's training tied to departmental and company goals?

For training to be truly effective, an employee's training must be aligned with the departmental goals and objectives established to meet the company's overall objectives. Once the departmental objectives are determined to support the goals of the company, the manager can begin to determine the knowledge gaps needed to be filled through training and the individuals that are chosen to fill the gaps. This way, allocating resources to be trained almost guarantees that there is a payback on the money and time invested.

Make sure the training is geared to filling in a gap, which if left void, would make it difficult for the department to meet its goals. Have the employee receiving the training write up a one or two page summary of the key points learned. This summary can then be distributed to other employees within the department for their education as well. Additionally, if the employee knows that he must write a summary on the course, chances are he will pay even closer attention to the course material. Stress to the employee ahead of time that one factor contributing to the department's success, is for the employee to be a champion of this new area. This will create an incredible sense of value and ownership for the individual and produce a much more productive employee.

If a mistake is made, is it viewed as a valuable learning experience?

No one likes a bully. And you can be sure; no one wants to work for one! When employee's, including managers, make mistakes there can be a valuable lesson learned on the experience. How one's boss handles the experience is the distinguishing factor between being a true mentor and being a bully.

Many individuals that supervise others react to a mistake by screaming, accusing, finger pointing, swearing, or criticizing, rather than taking the time to understand the situation and listening to the already disappointed individual. There may be a number of reasons why a mistake was made, and in many cases it simply is a result of a lack of training or understanding of one's job responsibilities. Use these types of circumstance to spotlight your high degree of professionalism and leadership. Long-term, this will result in an army of supportive soldiers behind you, rather than a mutiny and defections.

STRUCTURE

Structure or lack of, within an organization can greatly impact the behavioral tone of a company. Human Resources need to provide an organizational structure with policies and procedures to be strictly adhered to. Without these, an entity is severely limited in its growth potential. How many companies actually have a formal evaluation process in place, where employees and management can be held accountable? Are reference checks, drug testing, and background checks routinely performed on all new hires responsible for areas susceptible to high-risk, public scrutiny and theft of a material nature? Is your company in compliance with federal and state laws protecting an employee's rights? Is Human Resources viewed as a strategic part of the Company?

Setting the organizational ground rules, allows a Company to mitigate risks that can become rampant in a poorly managed business.

Does a formal evaluation process exist, and are employees and management held accountable?

Without regular and thorough reviews, employees and management are unable to be held accountable. This lack of accountability ultimately contributes to a company's own internal problems and inefficiencies. When developing evaluations it is essential that the one being evaluated fully understands his or her responsibilities, and has been thoroughly trained in each. Training simply instills confidence and enthusiasm in the individual. Although it may seem that there is but one or two key areas to measure an employee's performance on; a company should use eight to twelve main categories. Typical these would include productivity, attitude, technical skills, communication skills, time management, customer service, professionalism, quality of work, impact on profitability, and team orientation. Each of the above categories would be further broken down into job specific criteria.

It is the superior's responsibility to determine the relative importance of each category. For an employee measurement process to be truly effective, the feedback must occur more than just annually. As an added benefit, evaluations are a mentoring tool used to teach and cultivate the employee. At the same time it educates and develops the supervisor. In reality, most managers are simply not comfortable with providing feedback or have never been adequately trained in the process. Take the time for performance evaluations. If you do not, you will be doing a tremendous injustice to your business and its employees - your company's most valuable resources.

Are reference checks, drug testing and background checks performed on all key employees?

Once the candidate has passed through the interview process the company now must perform some key due diligence. Checking references, having the employee take a drug test, and performing a background check on potential management and key positions is a necessity in order to ensure that there are no major skeletons hanging out. Since it is so costly to hire new employees, get them trained, and then wait until then become efficient with their new position, a company must invest the money to guarantee that the potential employee is not lying and has no criminal charges, in addition to obtaining confirmation that the employee is a productive and enthusiastic worker.

Without proper due diligence, the company eventually ends up paying much more in dealing with problem employees. In small businesses, the problems that a troublesome employee brings to the workplace can be crippling to the business. Take the added precaution and get confirmation on the achievements of your next hires.

Are salaries and benefits comparable to market?

Whether it is an employer's or employee's market, when it comes to compensation and benefits it is critical for your company to be competitive with the market. Hiring good employees is tough enough, but retaining them is even more difficult. The better employees will stay if they know they are being treated fairly, and you can bet – they know what all the local competition is paying.

A company may elect to low ball their payroll and drive their personnel to an eighty-hour week, but as the saying goes, "you get what you pay for." You will be left with a miserable, unproductive, burnt out workforce, incapable of creativity, process improvement, and long-term loyalty. Determining whether your company is competitive with wages is really quite easy. Among the sources to ask are CPA's, attorneys, bankers, benefit brokers, the Chamber of Commerce, venture capitalists, and any association within your specialized field.

Is the speed of turnaround on applicants through the employment process quick?

Procrastinating during the hiring process will only lead to the top candidates being hired by other companies instead of yours. From the moment a classified is displayed on the Web or in the paper, your hiring team needs to be in an immediate response mode. The truly good candidates will simply not wait around weeks or months for a decision to be made. Additionally, the longer the search continues, the costlier it is to your company.

Hiring consumes a massive amount of resources and the quicker the process can be completed, the better for all parties involved. Have a hiring outline with the detailed steps involved in the process along with the responsibility of each individual and a timetable to complete each step. By streamlining the process you will have a far greater chance in hiring those top candidates.

Are non-hired employees sent a thank you correspondence note or email?

Treating people the way you would want to be treated is what it's all about. Only a minority of companies actually take the time to have some form of correspondence sent to the applicant stating that they have reviewed the resume and unfortunately the qualifications do not fit the job description.

"Thank you so much for the inquiry and we wish you well in your future endeavors," is a professional and courteous response. Remember, the candidates that you reject could be potential customers and most live within the local community. It is in the company's best interest to have the community and all rejected applicants respect the professionalism and courtesy of your business.

FUN

Fun in the workplace can provide a strategic advantage for your Company. At the end of the day, if an employee feels good about his job and company, he will remain a much more loyal and productive employee. At the root of determining whether an employee will be a positive or negative company spokesperson is the simple question - is the Company a fun place to work at? Can you name four fun things or events, excluding the Christmas party, over the last year at your company? Do employees take pride in their work? Does management enjoy their work?

I submit that there is a direct correlation between a productive and enthusiastic workplace, and a corporate culture where having fun is a part of the business. When one thinks of the best jobs he or she ever had, the ones that come to mind first are those companies that maintained a true sense of camaraderie and enjoyment within the workplace.

Can you name four fun things that happened last year - at work, or work related?

Over the years, when employees discuss the few companies that they worked for where they had positive experiences, one common denominator consistently jumps out – the employee had fun at work. When an employee likes his or her job, and company, he or she will tend to become much more productive, loyal, quality conscientious, and concerned about the overall state of the company.

In today's tight labor market, and with competitive pressures so great, having the perception of being a "fun place to work" oftentimes can be a distinct advantage. It is the employee masses that will ultimately determine the fate of a company, not the select few running it. For most employers it is human nature to look at wages as being the kingpin to employment. However, after time, the workplace culture plays a much greater role. Where is the company whose mission statement reads, "Make money and have fun"?

Does management enjoy their work?

When surveying people about why they liked working for a particular company, the common denominator is that the people had fun at the company. Going to your job can be more than picking up a paycheck and clock watching. Management needs to create a culture whereby people actually consider the workplace to be an enjoyable place where people are respected and trusted, and creativity and balance are encouraged.

One sign of whether the workplace is in fact, fun, is if management enjoys their work. Just look at the faces of the managers and one should be able to tell whether management is in a war or working for a professional company. It is up to management to foster a culture where workers take pride in their jobs and they come home each day to tell their families all the good things that happened at work; not just the bad.

Is employee turnover low?

If employee turnover is low, chances are your company's doing many things right. For those companies where turnover is high, management needs to look from within to assess the culture, processes, and demands place upon the workforce. Even worse than staff turnover, is high management turnover. When the heads of the departments and strategic decision makers start to leave, it is time for the employees to begin their job search. Oftentimes, management will leave because of the management style of the CEO.

If you are the CEO or founder and management turnover is an annual event, it is time to bring in a new CEO. The Board should pay close attention to management turnover as a key indicator of the CEO's ability to lead the company. To fully understand the organization's problems, create a simply survey form and have a number of the employees answer the questions. Look for a pattern and make some changes!

Are new employees introduced throughout the company?

Take the time to introduce new employees throughout the company. What a great way to start the employee and get his adrenaline going. It shows that you are thankful that he picked your place of employment, rather than a competitor. Before he arrives, use email to inform other workers, put up welcome signs in the lobby, hang notices in break room, and consider even having a monthly newsletter or flyer with a picture and background of the new hires.

It is their birthday; the first day of a new job. Make it one they will never forget!

Do employees take pride in their work?

If one takes pride in his work, chances are she is a much more productive employee. Workers can quickly become disheartened within a company in part because they just don't fit the corporate culture.

The corporate culture is developed and nurtured by management, but if the employees do not accept the culture then productivity will suffer because there is no pride in the hearts of the workforce. Pride can also suffer because of demographic issues surrounding the company and community. Be sure to pay close attention to the external demographics that could be effecting your employees' moral and productivity.

REWARDS

Rewards are what ultimately drive people. In most cases, a person's desire to achieve may never be fully realized without adequate incentives to properly motivate that employee. As a result, problems with: product and service quality, meeting time deadlines, customer service issues, resource utilization efficiencies, and many other areas, will negatively impact a company far greater than those companies where adequate performance rewards exist. Does your company have stock option, bonus, and profit sharing plans for everyone? Are employees able to provide input on their prospective benefits and rewards? Are rewards based upon the performance of an individual, her department and the company?

Companies need to give an employee a feeling of ownership, to share in the good times, and feel some of the pain in the bad times. Treat employees as if they are the most valuable resources your company has.

Is a bonus plan, ESOP, or profit sharing plan offered to all employees?

Although there are a number of ways to provide incentives to employees, by far the most effective is to make employees part owners of the business. Most often this is done with stock options, an ESOP, profit sharing, or bonuses. Off course the rewards chosen need to be of substance, not just some paltry sum. Rewarding employees based upon a company's performance, or creating a stock option plan, makes the employee a stakeholder in the company. He or she knows that as the company does better the employee will be rewarded. However, the company only does better if the employee produces.

Oftentimes it is only management and sales individuals that get incentives - companies ignore the masses. Yet it is the masses that will determine the overall success. A little ownership can go a long way! A sense of ownership by employees creates loyalty, which in turn creates a more productive worker. It is essential that employees feel like they are in the game. Give them some ownership – and make sure it is of substance.

Does the company communicate financial results to all employees?

Communicating financial results on a high level to all employees shows that management respects the workers enough to share confidential data with them. This gives the employee a sense of ownership and places responsibility on his or her shoulders. An employee will place a much greater reliance on management's word when seeing the results of poor performance on paper versus constantly being told we are not performing to standard.

Oftentimes many workers simply do not trust management, especially when the conversation is about profits and losses. Staff feels like they are being told that the company is losing money and because of that the business cannot afford to pay raises. When subordinates are called into a break room or conference room, for the purpose of being informed and treated as though they were management and owners, it is extremely positive and ultimately brings the company closer in its drive to excel.

Is there a suggestion box for employees to make recommendations?

Every company, no matter what the size and industry, should have an incentive system whereby for any recommendations made that are deemed to save the company a significant amount of money, the employee is given some monetary recognition. This is a WIN-WIN proposition!

Many companies believe that it is an employee's duty to try and make a process more efficient, think of a new service or product, or constantly be thinking about continuous improvement. That may be true, but the reality is many people are motivated by money. And for many front line workers, a reward of ten to one hundred dollars is significant, and will serve as sufficient incentive. Create a simple process whereby employees can be rewarded for their creative efforts and the company will be rewarded long term.

Is the environment one where the employees can approach their boss and CEO?

If employees feel like they can approach their boss and CEO, then they are much more apt to discuss problems, concerns and more importantly, discuss ideas on how to make something better. This creates a much more harmonious and productive workplace, which in turn creates a team-oriented atmosphere driven to achieve.

It is simply amazing how observant and knowledgeable front line employees are, and if they are allowed to express their views and ideas, the company will flourish. For those managers that believe they know best or their way is the only way – go back to school.

Does empowerment exist?

The level or grade of a staff or manager should determine the range of decision-making authority allowed the employee. It is simply not necessary to have a second person approve most corporate transactions. A company hires individuals because it feels they can do the job – so let them. Don't procrastinate over petty decisions, give your employees empowerment to make decisions.

In today's rapidly changing global environment the best companies are often nimble and can quickly change strategies, formulate solutions, and implement improvements. By empowering your employees, you possibly gain a competitive advantage over your competitors. Take advantage of your employees' capabilities and empower them.

Part 4 - Internal Processes

Internal Processes are the arteries of a business. Internal processes include:

1. **Marketing,**
2. **Sales,**
3. **Information Technology, and**
4. **Operations.**

If there is blockage within these four elements a business will rapidly deteriorate and eventually fold. For an enterprise to grow and prosper, it is critical to monitor and understand the variables and dynamics of these four elements. How is the communication flow between these departments? Do they understand how their departments add value and fit into the company's mission? Are departmental goals and objectives aligned with company-wide ones? Understanding the implications of these questions and your responses are critical to your business.

MARKETING

Marketing, if effective, is as powerful to a business as first impressions are to people. After all, image is everything! A lot of companies fail to see a difference between sales and marketing, and in fact discuss strategies within each discipline as if they are the same. A great sales force is limited without targeted marketing initiatives and a well-defined, executable marketing plan. Does your company perform sufficient marketing research to use in supporting the strategic plan and direction of the company? Is your company's marketing plan appropriately segmented with unique strategies for each segment?

Most senior management teams are not even aware of the potential threats and substitutes for the business' products or services. Without adequate marketing research on the industry, its competitors and the dynamics associated with rapidly changing technology within the company's space, the Chief Executive Officer could be leading the company down the wrong path. Where is your company most vulnerable? Understanding the implications of these questions and your responses are critical to your business.

Does the Company know the gain or loss of its market share (not revenue) over the previous year?

Most companies focus on revenue growth without ever taking the time to consider the year's market share gain or loss. In fact, most small businesses never even try to determine what their market share is. In the earliest phases of a company's life cycle it certainly is not as critical since the company is simply trying to prove out its business model and increase its customer base. However, as the company begins to gain traction in targeted markets, it needs to begin to better quantify both the overall size of the market and its respective share of it. Without this, a company is extremely vulnerable to the dynamics of the business market.

A company may be fooled into, say, increasing its capital expenditures for expansion because its revenues have increased greatly over the past year. Without knowing how much the actual market has increased, the company does not know whether they are losing or gaining market share. If the company learns it has in fact lost market share from the previous year, then it may be time to consider alternative strategies such as a possible sale of the business, changes to its pricing or marketing strategy, or a number of other possibilities. Taking the time to conduct meaningful market research is critical to a company's long-term success and growth.

Is there sufficient market research performed to support the marketing plan?

Many companies prepare a marketing plan without ever conducting any market research. Without research, the assumptions that one makes are purely a guess, and as a result so to is the corresponding sales forecast. If the forecast is a guess, then the operating budget is sure to be off.

It is absolutely imperative to conduct sufficient market research on the size of the market, the key competitors in the market, the expected growth rate of the market, potential substitute products or services soon to be introduced, pricing points, customer acceptance, and industry capacity to name a few. By researching this information, management can prepare a detailed marketing plan that is supported by industry data. Don't go blindly into execution of a marketing plan that is deemed for failure from the start because there is no support to the assumptions.

Are potential threats and substitutes identified and action plans formulated?

In today's rapidly changing world, a product that has gained market acceptance can become obsolete almost overnight. Technological breakthroughs in most industries occur in far greater numbers than even three or four years ago. Remember in 2000 to 2002, several technology behemoths took billion dollar inventory write-downs, only weeks after reporting quarterly results. Over the course of just a few weeks, additional inventory became obsolete because new technologies were introduced to the market.

Management must pay close attention within the marketplace and anticipate potential threats and substitutes. Industry trade shows are a great source of learning about new products and services and what lies ahead for the industry. By striving to create additional value for your customers you should reduce the probability of your customers switching to the newest and greatest. When threats and substitutes are identified, be sure to formulate action plans to mitigate the company's business risk. Lastly – act fast and decisively!

Are numerous marketing tools used?

Direct mail campaigns, telemarketing, billboards, newspaper advertisements, Internet banner ads, email campaigns, flyers, trade shows, company shirts, branding, television commercials, radio spots, and seminars are only some of the many marketing tools available to a company.

When attacking a market to gain market share, you need to surround your target and penetrate it from all angles. Get creative and use as many tools as your marketing budget will permit. Don't load up on one or two tools, it is much too risky and you take the chance that your marketing budget is blown on only two initiatives. Instead, try various schemes and track the results in each. Where is the money best spent? Is the average per unit cost of a customer acquisition reasonable compared to the product or service's selling price? Remember, the goal is simply not to generate revenue at any cost; the goal is to become profitable and to be able to scale the business model without incurring significant losses.

Are the distribution channels streamlined and effective?

If your company is having trouble generating sales, the problem may not totally be in your sales team or with the quality or cost of the product. How is your product or service ultimately being delivered to the customer? Do you use a reseller network, manufacturing representatives, retailers, the Internet, alliances, or subcontractors? Perhaps there is a problem with your key suppliers.

Take the time to monitor and evaluate your distribution channels. Make sure they are giving your account top priority. Which channels are producing? For the ones that are not – either demand changes or redirect to another channel. It could be a case of not providing enough incentives for a particular partner. Be sure that there is adequate compensation for your distribution partners and this should drive them to push your products.

SALES

Sales can be the driving force in creating a new global leader, or they can lead to a company's downfall. It is dependent on making smart sales! Unless you sell a totally off-the-shelve product, there should be some time committed to determining whether a particular customer makes sense - and not just for credit reasons. Also, does your company have a sales compensation structure allowing sales individuals to possible become the highest paid people in the organization? It should! Is the S.W.O.T. acronym frequently discussed and action plans formulated? Is a company's resources spent dealing with low volume, non-profitable customers whom require constant attention? What sales automation tools are used during the sales life cycle? Understanding the implications of these questions and your responses are critical to your business.

Remember, not all sales are good. And, the customer is in fact, sometimes wrong.

Has your company entered into several key strategic alliances?

It's all about networking and connections. Find some industry all-stars and attach your company's sails to them. By partnering with companies whose products or services compliment your own, it opens up distribution channels and it serves to get the word out that you exist. Additionally, it gives the perception that you are larger and stronger than you really are. A perfect analogy is the old Anderson Consulting commercial that had all the small fish swimming alone. Over time they began to swim together, and ultimately they formed the image of a shark by swimming in unison.

Don't waste time trying to hook the huge fish as a partner – it will take far too long. Instead, look for the up and coming industry second and third tier companies that will grow as you grow, and who also need partners like yourself. Remember, you simply will not be able to compete long-term if you try and execute alone.

Are there significant incentives that are based upon an achievable quota system and customer profitability?

If your salespeople are not highly compensated with variable incentive packages based upon a quota system and a customer's profitability to the company, then your company will probably fail to reach its fullest potential. More than anyone, sales individuals must be motivated, and the number one motivating factor is money!

Establish reasonable quotas and hold them accountable if they fail to meet the quotas. Meaning, after adequate training, they are on probation if they miss quota and if they miss for a second or third month, then they are let go. But if they hit their quotas, the payoff must be big! One of the most powerful contracts in business is a salesperson's incentive contract. If structured correctly, and you have hired the right individual and given her adequate training, you have a far greater chance of success, growth, and market share gain. One last point, the established quotas must be reasonable; otherwise, the sales individuals will give up before they even get started.

Is the acronym S.W.O.T. understood and discussed?

Strengths, weaknesses, opportunities and threats ("S.W.O.T.") can be discussed in relation to your competitors, the marketplace, or your products and services. It is a valuable acronym that keeps your sales individuals, as well as management, focused on the differentiators between your company and its competitors.

S.W.O.T. can help with developing sales and an overall business strategy. In addition, it can aid in helping with developing a marketing plan and even recruiting personnel. If you know where a company is vulnerable, then you can gain an advantage in the battle to gain market share. If you can anticipate potential threats to your business then you are able to develop contingency plans to mitigate the risk of such a threat. Discuss S.W.O.T. in your sales meetings and strategic planning meetings and your company will be better prepared with greater focus.

Are sales automation tools frequently used?

Using yellow note pads, pencils and other low-tech traditional supplies no longer cuts it in today's global dynamic environment. No matter what the industry and how big or small the market is, without using automated sales tools, a salesperson is at a tremendous disadvantage.

Companies should invest in arming their salesperson with the most cost effective tools available; similar to a soldier going into battle. These people are on the front lines – in the trenches fighting it out. They need to look professional, extremely efficient, and have all critical data and intelligence information available real-time, in the palm of their hands. It is surely one of the best investments a company can make; and the payoff can be huge.

Do sales and service members spend the majority of their time on larger, more profitable accounts?

Why spend time on low margin, resource-consuming customers? It makes little sense. Think about it. Do your competitors want to try and steal your unprofitable customers – no! They are looking to take your profitable ones. So the solution is simple – give your best customers the most attention and take care of their needs so they will stay with you.

When an employee leaves it is extremely costly to the company to find a replacement, train them and have them be ultimately loyal to the company. Even costlier to a company is losing a customer that is profitable. Everyone in a company should know the profitable customers and be ready to support them thoroughly. It is a classic 80% of your revenue and profits come from 20% of your customer base.

Take care of that 20% and your company will retain a competitive edge.

INFORMATION SYSTEMS

Information Systems are the backbone of a company. Failing to recognize this will leave a company at a huge disadvantage. Unless you are running a backyard lemonade stand, no single area of a company is as important as information systems. As such, absolute care and attention to detail must reside within this zone. Are routine backup and security procedures followed? Are technical enhancements, system upgrades, and any capital expenditure aligned with the company's strategic direction? Is the system user friendly, functional, and doesn't require high maintenance in relation to the system itself?

If one has ever lost data on a home personal computer, then one need only to multiply that nightmarish experience by 100, and you may be able to begin to understand the destructive impact on a business - should a similar problem occur. Have you taken every precaution in safeguarding your most valuable and intellectual assets? Understanding the implications of these questions and your responses are critical to your business.

Are routine backup and security procedures followed?

No matter how often one hears of the importance of having routine backup procedures surrounding the key information technology systems, one will never fully appreciate it until a company's data is lost. Certainly most individuals have lost some data that was being entered to a spreadsheet and the personal computer crashed before the file could be saved. Think of that frustration and time lost, then multiply that by one hundred or even one thousand and you might get a feel for the severity facing your company.

There is absolutely no excuse, none, for not having routine and secure backup procedures in place. This includes testing of the backup data. It is not enough to simply think one has backed up the system by copying files onto a disk or second drive. Occasional testing of the tape or second drive should be performed to ensure the accuracy and functionality of the backup. Without this testing you may be in for the surprise of your life.

Does a scaled down version of a disaster recovery and/or contingency plan exist?

Rarely do you hear of a small business that has expended the resources to prepare a disaster recovery plan. In most cases, a risk management decision is made that it is simply not worth the investment. A company would rather save the time and cost of preparing the plan, and take their chances that it is able to quickly and inexpensively return to business should a disaster occur. Terrorists, tornados, hurricanes, blizzards, earthquakes, computer hackers, and disgruntled employees are only some of the potential threats that can cause serious, immediate and permanent destruction.

At a minimum, all companies should prepare a five to ten page "emergency procedure checklist and policy summary" to implement during those "red alert" moments. Preparation of this type of report is cost effective, and does not require a significant amount of resources. When a disaster hits a small business, each day that goes by without being up and running increases the probability of the Company going out-of-business. If a business is not operational within three to four days, they will probably feel a significant financial strain. So when the robot states "Danger Will Robinson," be ready, and have a scaled down version of a disaster plan ready to execute.

Are enhancements, upgrades, and other purchases aligned with the strategic plan?

Hardware and software expenditures can drain huge amounts of capital and personnel time due to training, conversions and installations. For a company to truly remain competitive it must continue to invest in its infrastructure, and a large part of this infrastructure is information systems and technology. But how does one prioritize its technology wish list on such a limited budget? The answer lies in understanding where the market is headed, along with the strategic direction of the company. A business must align all significant, and most non-significant, capital information technology expenditures with the strategic plan and the corresponding initiatives.

Technology is a key ingredient to supporting the direction of a company and enabling it to meet its core objectives and goals. All departments can benefit from the proper technological upgrades and enhancements, just make sure that those upgrades make sense from a cost standpoint, and that they serve to help accomplish the departmental goals. In business, saving time on any facet of the business can lead to gaining a competitive advantage, and the more time saved – the greater your potential advantage.

Is the Company overly dependent on outside consultants?

Consultants, for the most part, look to get their foot in the door so they can become a part of the company. For some of them, they can gain incredible leverage over a business. Therefore, it is critical that the company does not allow itself to become overly dependant on the consultant. Should this happen, the company could ultimately pay a far greater price than that of alternative solutions. Be sure that part of the consultant's deliverables is documentation.

Most companies use outside information system contractors, because it allows much more flexibility for scheduling projects; however, IT contractors are notorious for submitting work – especially programming - that is not properly documented. Try and create a balance between internal and external resources. Off course that balance is largely dependent on the nature of the work, deadlines, and experience required. Nevertheless, do not allow consultants to dictate your needs or you will soon find that you had more needs than anyone imagined. This is one area where you want to verify with several references that the quality of work was outstanding and within the budget and timelines proposed.

Is the informational system user friendly, functional and requires only a little maintenance?

You can build the most complex and intelligent system there is, but if it is not user friendly and somewhat intuitive, the system will be ineffective and extremely costly to your organization. Additionally, the system should require a minimum amount of maintenance. If your staff is constantly working on the system due to upgrades, breakdowns, crashes, or backups, then chances are the utilization time by the users is significantly lower than what was intended. This translates into a costly overhead rate that will directly impact the company's profitability.

There is no need to build a rocket ship. A system that is highly functional and user friendly, with speed, is oftentimes more effective than a complex, highly integrated proprietary system. Management information system budgets can quickly escalate out-of-control. Stay within the parameters outlined upfront. The better a Company understands the market and its customers, the higher the probability that the budget will remain in tact.

OPERATIONS

Operations are all about following structured processes; staying focused on quality and customer service; and understanding the quantifiable metric between resource capacity and utilization. Does your company track its resource utilization to its resource capacity? Is the number of customer service representatives determined based upon the average number of daily complaints? Are delivery dates at 95% or better of promised dates? Are they even 50%? How is a new employee acclimated to her new job?

Oftentimes management assumes that things will just naturally happen, or they believe that problems will occur - so why try and prevent them? Taking time to plan, document, train, test, and communicate can mitigate a company's numerous potential operational setbacks - that are not typical within outstanding service entities.

Is resource capacity versus resource utilization frequently monitored and are action plans developed to minimize the gap between the two?

Whether your company is a manufacturing or service entity, being able to quantify the gap between capacity (how much is possible) and utilization (how much was produced), of either machinery or people, is critical. The gap's size should ultimately weigh heavily on the decision to whether, and when, to purchase more equipment or hire more individuals, or replace non-productive workers.

Without the ability to reasonably determine how many widgets can be produced in an hour, or how many vendor invoices can be entered into a system within an hour, a company will misappropriate its capital and human assets. Management needs to determine what the capacity constraints for all important processes are. Once completed, the next step is to monitor the gap on a regular basis so management can formulate solutions that serve to minimize the gap, and ultimately reduce costs. This makes for a far more productive and streamlined operation.

Is the Company's customer service considered to be outstanding?

The only way to achieve outstanding customer service is to have the entire company believing that outstanding customer service is essential to growth and profitable. Without this customer focused corporate culture, the entity will, in all likelihood – never be a long-term leader in its industry. With a customer-focused mentality, the company has a better chance than most of its competitors. Let's face it, there are not that many great customer service oriented companies. And for the ones that do exist, people remember them and refer their names to family, friends and business associates.

For a company to view the customer as paramount to its success, the Chief Executive Officer and his or her executive management staff must exhibit examples of delivering stellar service themselves. The CEO can talk all he wants to about having a "world class customer service organization", but the reality is unless he provides adequate resources, both technology and people, to make it happen, and holds all senior members of management accountable for service – it simply will not happen. If expectations are too great, your service reps will eventually rebel. For many companies, when business starts to slow or the economy hits a bump, service personnel and budgets are cut. This is the absolute worst time for making these cuts. During hard times, a company should place even more emphasis on customer service; and provide greater resources in support of customer service. For it is during these times that your competition is promising the world so that they too can continue in business. If you have taken the time, and provided the resources, to build a world-class service company – then you should have nothing to fear. Customers will remain extremely loyal if they believe you care and have delivered above their expectations.

Is there good housekeeping throughout?

All other things being equal, would you rather do business with a disorganized entity or one where people take pride in their work areas and regularly clean up? When a customer, supplier, interviewee, or stakeholder walks through a building or office and sees a mess, they immediately take note and wonder if this company or person is inefficient in other work habits. In today's extremely competitive environment, first impressions can become a deciding factor in ones decision to enter into a business relationship.

If you were going to a restaurant and saw a mess at the hostess' station, you probably would just walk out without ever eating. The same holds true in a grocery store, doctor's office, classroom, or any other location where people visit. Additionally, if housekeeping is an issue at work, chances are moral and productivity is very low. Ignore the individuals that state, "excuse my mess, I've been too busy to clean." Although they are busy trying to find things, they are not busy doing the things you pay them to do. Lack of organization is expensive. Clean things up!

Does the Company deliver a quality product or service as promised and on time?

Although it seems simple, getting a high quality product delivered on time is difficult to do for many companies. There are so many steps within the production and service cycle processes that can falter, that most companies just accept this as an ordinary part of business. Even more ludicrous is that many customers are conditioned to expect some type of product defect, time delay, or poor service. Try ordering a piece of furniture. This type of experience is precisely why the few companies continuing to focus on improving, and in some cases perfecting processes, can achieve an overwhelming competitive advantage within their markets.

High quality and meeting delivery dates are two key metrics that must be monitored on a monthly basis. The better a company does on these performance measures, the greater the chance of beating its competition over the long-term.

Is there good communications flow – both internally and externally?

For communication to be effective it needs a reaction similar to a stone being dropped in a calm pond; the ripples flow to all sides until it reaches the outer edge. Communication is an extremely powerful tool and if handled correctly, can be an energizing and unifying mechanism for employees. Make employees feel like they are part of a company by opening up the communication lines. This will lead to a more responsive, loyal and enthusiastic workforce.

For significant events or decisions, tell them why a decision was made. Communication is important for both good and bad issues. Be truthful and you will earn respect from the masses. Communication flow is also critical on an upward stream. Meaning, it is just as important to communicate to investors, the Board of Directors, the community, the press, customers, suppliers and other interested parties. Any party impacted by a decision should be informed on a timely basis in the most professional way possible.

Part 5 - Chief Executive Officer

Chief Executive Officer attributes are centered on the four fundamental areas associated with being a superior leader:

1. **Vision,**

2. **Management,**

3. **Communication, and**

4. **Planning.**

Although most entrepreneurs and founders are quick to place the title of CEO on a business card, the majority of these individuals are simply not the right person to lead the company into the next stage of the Company's life cycle. They often suggest that when the time is right, the company's reigns will be indeed turned over to an experienced CEO to lead the company in their next generation strategy. Unfortunately, the timing is never quite right.

The BASIC Business Model™ serves to identify the potential character flaws and executive limitations that will, without a doubt, be the root of a company's frustrating stagnation and underlying problems. The reason why so many companies fail can be directly traced to a CEO's inexperience and inability to step aside, learn and listen.

VISION

Einstein had it, so did Franklin, and so did many others - does your CEO have it? It is a critical virtue of a true leader. It can however; also hinder a business's ability to grow and prosper. Can your CEO make quick decisions, or is he a procrastinator? Is the CEO aware of the "big picture" or is she a perfectionist bogged down in a myriad of inconsequential details? Has the CEO proved that he or she can execute on the company's strategic plan, or are they continually redefining the mission and strategy?

There are countless executives that leave the managerial ranks of Corporate America to become founders of a start-up company, only to soon thereafter - falter. Typically these founders start a traditional type of business, franchise, or one that they have absolutely no experience in. They share the ability to take risk, but it does not make them a visionary. It is leading a company into the next stage of development that also will require vision and this is far more difficult.

Does the executive make quick decisions on most issues and does not procrastinate?

The ability by a senior manager to make timely decisions is critical to a company's success. Executives that continually ponder issues are simply doing great favors for their competitors. In today's radically changing environment, those companies and executives that regularly procrastinate will ultimately fail. It is simply not prudent to wait for all the facts before making a decision. Oftentimes, if a person has a sound business acumen and common sense, along with a high sense of professional ethics and morals, the decision made will be the right one. It is far better to make a decision than none at all. Certainly there is a correlation between the magnitude of the issue and its possible risks from a bad decision, and the amount of time that should be spent analyzing the issue and gathering supportive data. However, as Rodney said in the movie Caddie Shack, "While we're young!" Decide and then move on.

Is the executive a perfectionist?

One of the worst traits an executive can have is to be a perfectionist. Those that are, lack one of the most crucial skills in today's drastically changing environment – timely decision making. If an executive is resolute with gathering all the appropriate information, or obtaining a unanimous vote by all mangers on a key decision, or struggles with routine, simple processes or procedures, then the Company will have difficulty growing. One thing that is guaranteed in the business world, particularly in small businesses, is that mistakes will be made and there is absolutely nothing you could have done to prevent a lot of them. Perfectionism can also be extremely costly.

If you are worried about details, details and more details, you will be unable to compete in the ever- changing market. Pick your head up and look around. Nothing, except maybe brain surgery, needs to be one hundred percent perfect all the time. Another offshoot to perfection is that it drives all your subordinates crazy. Most will ultimately find a boss that is not so perfect; which means, they will find another company. Mistakes will be made – learn to tolerate the minor ones and move on.

Is the CEO experienced in delivering profits and growth?

It is one thing to have experience as an entrepreneur or CEO of a company, but it is immensely more important to have had experience in growing a profitable business. Anyone can run a business, and most run those businesses right into the ground. Consequently many start-up businesses fail because the founders' and CEOs simply do not have adequate experience. That is not to say that they are not tremendous marketers, sales people, managers, or technicians. In fact, most have at least one of those disciplines effectively covered. Be careful too, how you define growth. Being in business for ten years and having only one or two million in revenue is certainly not going to get you any entrepreneur of the decade award.

If your company is stuck in a rut, seek help. Talk with your Board of Directors, CPA, lawyer, management team, a mentor, another CEO, or a business coach or advisor. Don't let stagnation cripple your company's chance for success. You did a fantastic job on the front nine, now it's time for the difficult finishing holes. Seek some help to deliver the profits and growth that you have so long desired.

Does the executive consider the business complex?

Executives that state "Well you don't understand, we have a complex business in a difficult market," simply should not be running companies. First of all, every market is difficult to operate in – the trick is to out smart and out think your competition. Secondly, and more importantly, businesses are only as complex as management makes them out to be. It all boils down to the nuts and bolts: Business 101. If the company's foundation is solid and the core processes are effective and in place; then the company should be able to survive explosive growth. If management believes the business to be complex then management is not creative enough or they are simply out-of-their league and need to work elsewhere.

Just because there are more zeros behind larger company numbers does not make that business more complex either. Cut through the layers and focus on the mechanics of what business goals the company is trying to accomplish. Next, have management leverage your company's core competencies to achieve these goals. Slash all the fat, unnecessary overhead and non value-added steps, and you should be left with an extremely manageable, streamlined, agile, non-complex business. Just be certain that you are slicing off the fat – not the meat.

Is the executive excellent at leveraging the company's "core competencies"?

What are the core competencies of your company? Perhaps it is the distribution channels, the technology, your ability to be lost-cost provider, your management team, product development, turn-around time, or quality. Whatever they are, is your company doing everything

possible to leverage these to increase its competitive position? If not –
you need to develop a strategy to ensure that the core competencies are
utilized.

Some companies may be good at many parts of the business,
without being great in any one or two areas. That is okay. Most
companies are very good at one or two things, but barely get by in the
other areas. For these companies they must leverage off their strongest
attributes in order to gain a competitive advantage. If you have the best
distribution channels in the industry, then determine what other
complimentary products or services could be offered through these
channels. Whether those products or services come from other
companies or yours doesn't matter. If your channels are the core
competency within your business, then continue to feed those channels
with products or services. The result will be more revenue and higher
margins flowing through to the bottom line.

PLANNING

Planning - it enabled Lombardi to win the first two super bowls,
and Schwarzkopf to win a war. Does your CEO have a written plan on
how to win at business? It is a critical virtue in a true leader. Without
adequate planning, a business will lose the long-term battle to its
competitors. With an executable, well laid out plan, the chances of
winning vastly improve. In business, planning goes well beyond having
an updated strategic plan. That blueprint must be followed by
departmental plans that are aligned with the strategic goals and
direction of the company. Departmental plans must then be tied to
individual action plans that enable a company to hold employees

accountable. This accountability will increase the company's chances of winning.

Successful executives understand how crucial it is at executing according to one's plan. For those that fail to plan altogether, they never stand a chance. Planning is a fundamental ingredient to a business's prosperity and absolutely paramount to its continued existence. Take the time to plan . . . your company's future depends on it!

Are departmental action plans aligned with the strategic plan and monitored?

Once the strategic and/or business plan is complete, it is necessary to prepare departmental action plans that align with the company's overall plan. Without these, a large portion of the efforts associated with developing the strategy and overall company blue print will eventually be wasted. Departmental action plans serve to ensure that all the disciplines of the business are on "the same page." This includes sales, marketing, operations, information systems, finance and human resources. It also allows for better accountability of managers and their departments.

In addition, if a department achieves its goals and objectives, then the company is guaranteed to benefit as well. Every facet of a business ultimately leads to the success or failure of a business. Employees also gain an understanding and appreciation of how their job creates value within the overall entity, which in turn makes for a more productive worker. Take the time to make sure each department is working towards a common mission, and develop departmental action plans.

Do senior managers have individual action plans that are used to hold them accountable?

The CEO is the one person that must hold all senior management members accountable. This is not a responsibility that can be delegated to anyone else; it is one of the CEO's primary duties. And the best tool for holding management accountable is to prepare individual action plans for all members of senior management.

The action plans should be aligned with the strategic plan objectives of the business. However, the plans and goals need to be realistic otherwise the managers will feel defeated and be truly unmotivated. Should the individual fail to achieve his or her objectives then the CEO should take immediate action. Without enforcing accountability, management will not have a sense of urgency and some may take advantage of the situation. The CEO needs to set an example for all and if performance is lacking, people need to be terminated.

Is there a succession plan?

Who will take the reins when the time comes? Don't take anything for granted, as it is up to the CEO and Board of Directors to decide on the CEO's successor and the qualifications desired of the candidate. If you think that you are in it for ten years then start looking at candidates in the sixth year. Find someone to bring in and groom for a couple of years before the transition is made. Hiring early on in the process also gives you sufficient time to find another candidate if the original candidate has not worked out.

With the years of blood, sweat and tears that you endured to grow your business, it is critical that you have a succession plan in place to ensure that the company survives and your family and employees are able to obtain the monetary rewards from the next generation of executives. Don't procrastinate on such a serious matter.

Does the executive prepare a weekly and monthly priority list?

As employees should prepare weekly and monthly plans, so too should executives. An executive has a myriad of challenges, responsibilities, and high impact decisions to make. To make matters even worse, these issues can change in importance on a daily basis based upon business dynamics. Therefore, it is absolutely critical for the executive to have a prioritized list covering customers, investor relations, management, employee communications, etc. Without a written list, the executive would be forced to crisis manage all situations.

Taking control of ones schedule will enable the executive to keep the company on its course and focused on strategic initiatives.

Does the executive have a plan to balance his or her personal life and work?

Without a balance in his or her life, the executive will ultimately fall short of maximizing his abilities. In addition, the lack of balance will place enormous stress on the executive, as he will be consumed with work, which in turn will impact all other members of management and their subordinates. Lastly, this imbalance will alienate most of the workers since they will feel like the executive is unable to relate to their own desire to balance work and family life.

Although the executive may say we need to live and breathe work 24 hours a day, that intense attitude will ultimately lead to the departure of many highly effective employees and managers. The fact remains that there is more to life than just work, and for the executive that understands this, the rewards include a much more productive, loyal and enthusiastic workforce. This is turn, leads to an improved competitive position within your marketplace. If the masses of employees are happy – they will produce. It is time for the executive to set an example and gain a manageable balance between work and living. You will be a much happier and healthier person as a result.

COMMUNICATION

Communication - there are only a handful of great communicators, such as King and Lincoln, whose communications have the power to impact even more of the world's population as generations pass. But what about within a small business, is your CEO capable of positive and insightful communications to management and the company's employees? Or, does he or she prefer to hide behind an office door? Can you honestly say that your company's CEO is an honest, trustworthy, well-respected person? If not, why do you continue working there? Does the CEO excel at mentoring, motivating, and managing people?

Communication, whether verbal or written, is the most powerful form of expressing oneself and one's character. In today's real-time business environment, emails and instant messages are rapidly sent between parties without thinking of the consequences, never mind the ever-lasting trail of character flaw evidence. For a company to succeed and prosper; positive and constructive communication is critical. The message is long-time remembered; not the time it took to send it.

Is the executive an excellent mentor?

Chances are if you work for a truly great manager, at one time or another he or she had a gifted mentor to help show them the way. I submit that there is a lot less good managers than there was a decade or two earlier, and the reason has to do solely with the way the business environment has changed over this period. Today's business setting is structured to function at a much quicker pace and to be reactive to a constant evolution of market dynamics. In this type of venue many executives consider it nearly impossible to take precious time away to mentor subordinates.

Mentoring, nurturing and coaching are a lost art. Because of this, many of the current generation of executives have never been adequately trained on the skills needed to mentor and lead individuals. The fallout will become even worse with the next generation of managers. The cost effect on a company cannot be quantified. Lost productivity, poor decision making and problem solving capability, lack of loyalty, and weak supervisory skills are just a few of the ramifications from not having a sound mentoring program in place. To make matters worse, think of how poorly the training is for second and third tier employees. So for the few executives that actually take the time to mentor their protégés, the company is gaining a long-term competitive advantage. Many of those protégés will then take the time for their subordinates. Soon, you have transformed the corporate culture of the business into a mentoring factory, whose employees are better skilled for the numerous challenges that lie ahead.

Does the CEO do an effective job of motivating management and staff?

Where would Martin Luther Jr., General Patton, JFK, Vince Lombardi, and a host of other great leaders be without being able to motivate their following? Having the ability to motivate is an essential quality of any would-be leader. The ability to motivate is not to be interpreted as an ability to scream, pound fists, threaten and use other bullying tactics. They simply do not work and serve only to portray the boss as someone that has little self-confidence and leadership abilities. Why would anyone want to be associated with a person with those qualities? Most budding superstars simply end up leaving for a competitor.

Motivation is about setting realistic goals, explaining why those goals are important, how the individual plays an important role in achieving those goals, using positive reinforcement during difficult times, and praising the efforts of the team when the goals are met. Should the goals not be met then a reassessment should be performed. Oftentimes the reason for not meeting goals is due to a lack of leadership talent, inadequate resources, or the misguided direction and vision of the executive. Or perhaps it is simply that the goals are unrealistic and unachievable to begin with. People and organizations can overcome enormous odds if they are nurtured and motivated to reach the end. The human spirit will endure if it is not being attacked by ones boss. Remember, you are on the same team as the masses - so function as one!

Does the CEO "walk the talk"?

If you are adamant about having a world-class customer service organization, or creating a culture that is based upon open communications throughout, or perhaps you have no tolerance for people that do not respect others professionally, then remember it all starts at the top and you are the individual under the spotlight on center stage.

It is one thing to talk about an issue that you are steadfast about, but it is entirely another to demonstrate on a consistent and public basis that you backup your theories, morals, concepts and ideologies. Speaking out of both sides of the mouth will not earn you any respect among the troops and will only serve for them to inquire about your true intentions. Show your subordinates that you mean what you say by example, not just words, and they will unite in their desire to make it happen.

Does the CEO listen to her managers and staff?

Good listeners can make great managers. On the other hand, managers that are constantly interrupting or failing to understand the communications being presented them are limiting the company's potential and that of their employees. When given an opportunity, most people are extremely vocal and honest, but if they feel like the other party is disinterested or is constantly cutting them off in mid sentence, then they will hold their creative ideas and solutions to themselves.

Few managers succeed over the long-term if they have poor listening skills. If they would rather listen to themselves talk and feel that only their views matter, then they should move to a company that embraces a dictatorship environment. Of course, this type of environment will be doomed for failure. Listening skills may be the most important communication skill there is. Next time a situation presents it – sit back, listen and take notes. Even silence is better than hearing the constant rhetoric of an executive restating his personal agenda. Remember there is much more pent up creativity and solutions in the masses than in one person.

Are there weekly management meetings?

Without weekly management meetings, the team and their coach – the CEO, have no way of knowing what progress is being made, what new obstacles were encountered, and what opportunities have arisen. It is critical for all senior members of the team to be involved in this weekly communication meeting, because a new opportunity for sales maybe a potential problem for operations. In most cases, an opportunity for one or two departments usually means tremendous challenges for others. Weekly meetings should be long enough to have each senior member talk for up to fifteen minutes, if necessary. If certain topical areas consume a significant amount of time, then that subject area should be tabled for a separate meeting.

It is appropriate for someone to take minutes for documentation purposes and to hold people accountable for promises made. For a company to be successful over the long-term, it is absolutely critical that all managers be brought into the loop whenever new significant data comes to light. Otherwise, some managers will make decisions that ultimately create forest fires that other managers are busy putting out. The best way to avoid crisis management is to have weekly communication meetings with your senior staff members, but remember to listen to all objections before you leap into what appears on the surface to be a "can't miss" opportunity. Remember every company has limitations in its operational capacity, available capital, personnel resource utilization, and its ability to deliver what is expected.

MANAGEMENT

Management - Kennedy was a master at it, as was Jack Welch. Are you as effective at managing within a small business as they were within global organizations? A company vastly decreases its chances of growth and prosperity when top executives within a company are not skilled in managing people. It all starts with the management team being unified and working to support the CEO's vision and the company's mission statement. Additionally, the management team must be technically sound within their functional areas, but not necessarily experts on their industry segment. How is the chemistry between your CEO and the management group?

Most important are the simple qualities of trust and respect between the CEO and the management team, and having this trust and respect filter down into all layers of a company. Does your CEO exhibit credibility and integrity, or does he or she use bullying tactics to manage? Nothing is more telling on whether a company is well run, than watching the interaction between a CEO and the company's employees.

Is the CEO honest, trustworthy, and well respected by staff and management?

If the CEO has not gained the trust of his/her subordinates, then the company will be severely derailed from its path to success. Chances are, if the employees don't trust the CEO neither will the customers, investors, alliance partners and other stake holders. Nothing symbolizes a business more than the image and character of its CEO. Companies talk of the value in branding their products – well the branding of the CEO is even more important.

The CEO is on the stage and if the audience feels like they are being deceived then they will walk out. Being honest and trustworthy will serve to gain the confidence of the troops while at the same time increasing their morale. The masses will believe and work even harder to make the dreams and mission a reality. Don't go around blowing smoke! Your better employees will immediately see through this and end up going over to the competition.

Is there good chemistry between the CEO and management team?

If the CEO doesn't get along with her management team and vice-versa, then the company has problems that it must immediately rectify. If the chemistry is poor, then the team will not be able to effectively function as a unit. Without this unity, goals will not be achieved and the company will ultimately suffer in its path to future growth and profitability. Additionally, it is extremely important for the members of management to get along. That doesn't mean that they need to have cookouts on the weekends together, but rather they must be able to work towards common goals, helping and supporting each other for the good of the company. If this is not the case, then changes must be made within the ranks.

This does not mean shoot the messenger of bad news. Sometimes the management setting is one where a few managers have become friends and will therefore not challenge each other at business. This does the company no good. There may be one or two managers that consistently talk about breakdowns in the processes and appear to be critical of others, but in actuality, they are only pointing out true problems within the company. The other managers may view this individual as a threat to their own territory and thus, push the CEO to move out the individual through reorganization. What should have been done is for the CEO to look beyond the person and decide whether the comments were valid. If so, the managers that felt threatened should have been replaced. Chemistry is critical, but be sure that the inferior players are not ganging up on your true superstars.

Is the management team knowledgeable in their respective areas?

You hire managers because they have technical experience within their business disciplines, but what happens if you determine that they do not have sufficient experience to handle the challenges confronting the business when it gets to the next level? The CEO has to be able to continually reassess a manager's capability as the company grows. The same holds true for the necessity of the Board of Directors' to reassess a CEO's ability.

If it is determined that the manager does not have the technical expertise required to perform the duties of her position, then there are three solutions. Firstly, is there training that can be provided to expand her skills? If practical and the timing are within a reasonable period, then this is the best solution because it shows that the company continues to promote from within and it cares about its employees. Secondly, there is the option of repositioning the manager within the respective department, or within another department, as a director rather than say Vice-president, and hire someone with larger company experience. Lastly, there is the possibility that it is in both parties best interest to depart. If this is the case, be sure that the situation is handled professionally and with some type of severance package. The way you handle this will be an example to the other managers. If they believe that the departing manager received a bad deal, then they might start looking to leave on their own timeline, leaving the company with many holes to fill.

One last point; if managers do possess the necessary skills to run their departments then get out of their way. Support them in their decisions, provide them with the necessary resources and praise them for their achievements.

Does the CEO trust and support the management team?

If the CEO does not trust and support the management team then either the entire management team should be let go or the CEO should go. Of course there is an alternative solution; the CEO could find a business coach that would be able to mentor him why it is so important to be able to trust your managers and support them in their decisions. If this is a reoccurring problem with the CEO, (i.e. he or she has never been able to trust people), then the CEO needs to immediately take some steps to becoming a better leader or look for a successor. Most Boards of Directors will not accept this, because there are plenty of trusting CEOs in the marketplace.

It is also less expensive to the company to hire a new CEO than to hire six new managers. A CEO has to accept the fact that the majority of managers will, over a majority of the time, make the right decision. No one is perfect and everyone makes mistakes – so accept it, support them, offer guidance, and move on. If you cannot trust your people then you should not be in business. This is one of the main reasons why entrepreneurs never grow their companies past being a micro-sized company. They want to be involved in every decision and have final say on all aspects of the business. Creation of an idea is only the first step; execution of that idea or concept into a market dominating position is more than a step – it's a leap and journey that few founders ever get to experience.

Does the management team support the CEO's vision and mission?

If the team does not support the CEO's directed course for the company, then the company has severe problems and a remedy must immediately occur. Oftentimes a CEO will believe that the vision and mission are so obvious that anyone that can't see it must be incompetent or not understand business. However, if the entire management team seems to be saying, "I think we should head North, and the ship is going South," then you might want to recheck your compass. A possible suggestion is to find a team of two or three independent knowledgeable business people that could serve as an arbitration team. If you had an outside Board of Directors, then it would ultimately be their decision; but if you don't, then find some people that are respected within the business community and propose the question to them.

It is imperative that the management team agrees with the CEO on the vision and mission of the company. If the CEO says we are going to hit singles and bunts to score a run, but management is swinging for the fences – then the game is over!

21. Your Company's Future

It is up to the executive to get things done. Don't be looking for the latest and greatest consulting buzz trends to implement. Stick to what you learned long ago – the **BASICs**. Use the *BASIC Business Model* ™ within your business. Tweak it. There may be other critical but simple questions to ask. Formulate easy to implement strategies, processes and/or solutions. Don't get bogged down in the minutiae – you simply don't have the time. But in the end – you must be proactive and look at all twenty components of the Model. Start with going to Appendix A - now.

Good luck to your company and yourself. It really shouldn't be that strange and scary within your business.

The End

Michael S. Boch, CPA

APPENDIX A – *How Healthy is Your Business?*

Get a **BASIC Business Checkup™** now! Simply answer the questions below as they relate to your Company. For each "no" answer, except for the questions that state that "no is positive", check the box and then count the total number of boxes checked. You can then grade yourself based on the one hundred questions. Use the different scores by segments to help prioritize the company's weaker areas. For narrative on each question, refer to the appropriate chapter within the book. Have other managers answer the same questions to substantiate your thinking. If appropriate, delegate to the management group the various areas that received a "no" and have them develop action plans. Your Company will be far better of with as few "no" responses as possible. Good luck and get started now! You owe it to your company and yourself.

Baseline Factors:

- ○ Does the CEO meet annually with key customers?
- ○ Are key accounts surveyed annually?
- ○ Does any customer account for greater than 25% of total revenues, or do any two customers account for greater than 40%? **(A no answer is positive)**
- ○ Is the customer list pruned annually?
- ○ Is the customer sometimes wrong?
- ○ Can senior management and the sales team members name the top five competitors?

- ○ Can the CEO and sales team members name three strengths of each major competitor?

- ○ Is management open to acquisitions with competitors?

- ○ Does senior management bad-mouth the competition? **(A no answer is positive)**

- ○ Is the Company susceptibility to global competition?

- ○ Has the company developed and implemented an overall grading system for major suppliers?

- ○ Is annual financial information on major suppliers requested?

- ○ Does the Company monitor subcontractor utilization?

- ○ Is low cost often the most important issue when selecting a supplier? **(No, is positive)**

- ○ Are there emergency back-up suppliers available?

- ○ Is there a plan to deal with the greatest demographic issue facing the company?

- ○ Is the Company's product or service considered to be value-added?

- ○ Is there union activity? **(A no answer is positive)**

- ○ Is the "word on the street" positive?

- ○ Does senior management consider the business to be complex? **(A no answer is positive)**

Accounting:

- ○ Are cash flow projections prepared on a 3, 6 and 12 month basis, and revised quarterly?

- ○ Is there sufficient cash and capital to weather a financial storm?

- ○ Does any one shareholder own greater than fifty percent? **(No, is positive)**

- ○ Are there several viable options on raising emergency funds?

O Is the method used to value the company consistent with that used within the industry?

O Have you done a complete background check on the Controller and/or CFO?

O Is the number one accounting person a Certified Public Accountant ("CPA")?

O Is the number one accounting person heavily involved in business decisions?

O Is the top accountant a "yes" person? **(No, is positive)**

O Is there an adequate segregation of duties within key account areas?

O Is a key performance indicator report, monitoring all the key success factors within each department, prepared monthly?

O Is the month end close by the fifth business day?

O Are monthly reporting packages delivered timely to management?

O Is there a reliable forecasting model and process in place?

O Is there an accurate cost accounting system?

O Is an annual operating budget prepared and are monthly meetings held to discuss variances?

O Does the company utilize at least three key external controls?

O Are monthly reconciliations performed on all key accounts on a timely basis?

O Does the CEO understand how to interpret the monthly financial results?

O Are capital expenditures financially justified?

Staffing:

- Does the CEO consider training critical to the long-term success of the company?

- Are training costs actually budgeted for in the annual operating plan?

- Do key staff, managers and the CEO have annual training?

- Is an individual's training tied to departmental and company goals?

- If a mistake is made, is it viewed as a valuable learning experience?

- Does a formal evaluation process exist, and are employees and management held accountable?

- Are reference checks, drug testing and background checks performed on all key employees?

- Are salaries and benefits comparable to market?

- Is the speed of turnaround on applicants through the employment process quick?

- Are non hired employees sent a thank you correspondence note or email?

- Can you name four fun things that happened last year - at work, or work related?

- Does management enjoy their work?

- Is employee turnover low?

- Are new employees introduced throughout the company?

- Do employees take pride in their work?

- Is a bonus plan, ESOP, or profit sharing plan offered to all employees?

- Does the company communicate financial results to all employees?

- ○ Is there a suggestion box for employees to make recommendations?

- ○ Is the environment one where the employees can approach their boss and CEO?

- ○ Does empowerment exist?

Internal Processes:

- ○ Does the Company know the gain or loss of its market share (not revenue) over the previous year?

- ○ Is there sufficient market research performed to support the marketing plan?

- ○ Are potential threats and substitutes identified and action plans formulated?

- ○ Are numerous marketing tools used?

- ○ Are the distribution channels streamlined and effective?

- ○ Has your company entered into several key strategic alliances?

- ○ Are there significant incentives that are based upon a quota system and profitability?

- ○ Is the acronym S.W.O.T. understood and discussed?

- ○ Are sales automation tools frequently used?

- ○ Do sales and service members spend the majority of their time on larger, more profitable accounts?

- ○ Are routine backup and security procedures followed?

- ○ Does a scaled down version of a disaster recovery and/or contingency plan exist?

- ○ Are enhancements, upgrades, and other purchases aligned with the strategic plan?

- ○ Is the Company overly dependent on outside consultants? **(No, is positive)**

○ Is the informational system user friendly, functional and requires only a little maintenance?

○ Is resource capacity versus resource utilization frequently monitored and are action plans developed to minimize the gap between the two?

○ Is the Company's customer service considered to be outstanding?

○ Is there good housekeeping throughout?

○ Does the Company deliver a quality product or service as promised and on time?

○ Is there good communications flow – both internally and externally?

Chief Executive Officer:

○ Does the CEO make quick decisions on most issues and does not procrastinate?

○ Is the CEO a perfectionist? **(No, is positive)**

○ Is the CEO experienced in delivering profits and growth?

○ Does the CEO consider the business complex? **(No, is positive)**

○ Is the CEO excellent at leveraging the company's "core competencies"?

○ Are departmental action plans aligned with the strategic plan and monitored?

○ Do senior managers have individual action plans that are used to hold them accountable?

○ Is there a succession plan?

○ Does the CEO prepare a weekly and monthly priority list?

○ Does the CEO have a plan to balance his or her personal life and work?

- ○ Is the CEO an excellent mentor?

- ○ Does the CEO do an effective job of motivating management and staff?

- ○ Does the CEO "walk the talk"?

- ○ Does the CEO listen to her managers and staff?

- ○ Are there weekly management meetings?

- ○ Is the CEO honest, trustworthy, and well respected by staff and management?

- ○ Is there good chemistry between the CEO and management team?

- ○ Is the management team knowledgeable in their respective areas?

- ○ Does the CEO trust and support the management team?

- ○ Does the management team support the CEO's vision and mission?

How did you do? For an easier way to print off your results and obtain a complete narrative visit www.thebusinessclinic.com and get a BASIC Business Checkup™ or BASIC Business Examination™. Should you have any questions, please call 919-844-3201.

I wish you good luck and good fortune.

Warm Regards,

Michael S. Boch

www.ingramcontent.com/pod-product-compliance
Lightning Source LLC
Chambersburg PA
CBHW022023170526
45157CB00003B/1330